BASIC BERKONOMICS

Over 100 powerful insights for starting, growing and successfully exiting your entrepreneurial business

Dave Berkus and eleven entrepreneurial expert friends

Published by: *The Berkus Press, a DBA of David Berkus*

For corrections, company/title updates, comments, or any other inquiries, please e-mail DBerkus@berkus.com

First Printing, 2012
10 9 8 7 6 5 4 3 2 1

ISBN number 978-1-300-181958

Some of the material in this book was serialized, previously published in the blog, **Berkonomics.com**, by the author.

Groups may order copies of the book at a group discount by contacting Dave Berkus at 626-355-5375, or at <u>dberkus@berkus.com</u> .

Throughout this book, the Cambria type font was used for headlines, and text was set using the Calibri font.

The views expressed by the individuals in this book do not necessarily reflect the views shared by the companies they are employed by (or the companies mentioned in) this book. The employment status and affiliations of authors with the companies referenced are subject to change.

Contents

INTRODUCTION

What's so basic about entrepreneurism? How do you become a *power* entrepreneur? How much of it is in your genes and how much can be learned? This book is your resource for your life of entrepreneurism, from start to successful exit, supplying important insights into the entire process. You may have the entrepreneurial gene, but the things you'll learn from this book will surely make you better equipped to grow your business, handle issues along the way, and add value that will make the real difference when you finally position to sell your interest and close this chapter.

In addition to the many insights I offer along with stories from my own experience, I have asked twelve of my very well-versed friends to contribute some of their stories and insights for this book. You'll be drawn into the plight of the entrepreneur who lost everything when his business failed, and the investor who carefully analyzed what went wrong with that business. You'll appreciate the detailed lists that guest authors give to help you organize presentations, protect partnerships, raise money, or prepare for an exit. Other experienced entrepreneur and investor friends who've volunteered short insights for this book write about their expectations for your business plans, your presentations, and your preparedness.

Several of these insights are marked *"Back to basics,"* highlighting the fact that some readers will find these a bit too elementary, and others will want to pay particular attention.

You may be a reader of my weekly BERKONOMICS blog, short insights sent by email, RSS, social media posts and re-postings around the world. This book contains more than 100 such short insights for effective business management, and is a continuation of the previous two BERKONOMICS books, each with 101 original insights, based upon my over fifty years of experience as an entrepreneur, board member and angel investor. This book completes the series of three, moving from this volume, "Basic," to previous volumes - "Berkonomics" and "Advanced."

The original books, and the excerpts that were subsequently published in the blog (www.berkonomics.com), are routinely read, tweeted and re-tweeted, posted and re-posted, fed to RSS readers, crawled and indexed, forwarded by email, downloaded and reprinted by tens of thousands of individuals, web and print journalists and entrepreneurial-focused organizations. I've even extracted stories from these insights, and have created a series of keynote addresses under the subject of "Finding Alpha" (unusually high angel investment returns.) Everyone likes to hear stories about others who have gone before them, doing well or behaving badly.

So we'll tell even more stories in this book, all to make more points about starting, building, growing, and ultimately perhaps selling your interest in the business.

You can pick up this book and read one or many of these insights at a time, and in any order that suits you. There are six general subjects, arranged to help you navigate through those that are most urgent to you at any given time, or just to know where in the map you have landed at any given time.

It's been a pleasure meeting thousands of readers who come up to me with comments about the books or blog, as I travel the world giving keynotes on corporate governance, building businesses, finding great investment returns, or tracking the latest trends in technology for entrepreneurs and investors. Hello again to each of you.

Feel free to mark up this volume and return to your marked pages as a reminder to act, not just read. Treat this book as a tool, an ever-present coach, reminding you to do more, do better, do your best.

Dave Berkus
Arcadia, California

"Where there is mystery, there's margin. Create what others cannot. That's a simple key to building a sustainable, profitable business."

- *Dave Berkus*

A GRATEFUL NOD TO THE CO-AUTHORS OF THIS BOOK

This is my fifth book, and with derivatives, the sixteenth publication from *The Berkus Press*. I am very fortunate to have expert help this time from some very smart friends in the business, each of whom has volunteered to contribute one or more insights for this book, directly from their personal experience of working as an entrepreneur or with entrepreneurs.   Here's a special thanks to these friends, whose contributions are definitely for your benefit.

- ***Dave Berkus***

Here is a short several sentence introduction to each and the page numbers where you'll find them inside this book.

Dave Berkus *is an internationally recognized super-angel investor, author and keynote speaker. See full bio in the back of this book.*

William De Temple *is a seasoned executive with experience in turn-around and start-up ventures. As CEO of Maximize Management, Inc., he oversees work with turn-around and growth company clients nationwide. William is also founder of The Enterprise Training Academy.*   P.108, 183

Eric Greenspan *is a consummate entrepreneur and blogger. His company, Make It Work, was a significant presence in California major metropolitan areas for over a decade, and attracted numerous rounds of angel investment over the years.*   P.177

John Huston *is founder and manager of the 300+ member Ohio TechAngel Funds and a past Chairman of both the Angel Capital Association and the Angel Resource Institute.*   P.170, 181

Berni Jubb *was an Inc.500 entrepreneur, after years as a senior marketing manager of a large computer company. He regained his senses, and now runs a small resort and restaurant in Costa Rica.*   P.165

Bill Payne *has been actively involved in angel investing since 1980, funding over 50 companies and mentoring over 100 more. He is the* recipient of the coveted "Hans Severiens Award form the Angel Capital Association, its highest honor. *P.67, 71, 72*

Frank Peters made his money writing software for Wall Street. Today he is best known as the host of the Frank Peters Show, delivered via the web each week to tens of thousands of entrepreneurs, angels and VCs worldwide. Frank speaks and networks at angel events around the world. *P.46, 152*

Basil Peters is perhaps the best known name in the world of early stage company exits. His groundbreaking book, "Early Exits" has become a textbook for angel groups and entrepreneurs throughout the world. His Strategic Exits Corporation provides M&A advisory services, and he is much in demand as a speaker at angel and entrepreneur events worldwide. *P.66, 173, 174*

Eric Rhoads is an entrepreneur founder of several businesses and is chairman of Streamline Publishing, a media company with conferences, print and electronic publications, video, and books. *P.179*

J.J. Richa is a successful entrepreneur and technologist giving back to the entrepreneurial community in many ways, including his weekly Internet TV program on entrepreneurism, and participation in several mentoring programs. *P.24, 35, 55, 58, 60, 69, 74, 144, 158*

David S. Rose: Described by BusinessWeek as a "world conquering entrepreneur" and by Forbes as "New York's Archangel", David is a former Inc. 500 CEO, serial entrepreneur and the founder of New York Angels. He is the founder and CEO of Gust, the angel financing platform used by over 50,000 accredited investors in 1,000 angel groups and venture capital funds to collaborate with over 250,000 entrepreneurs in 95 countries. *P16*

David Steakley, a past President of the Houston Angel Network, is a reformed management consultant. He is an active angel investor, and he manages several angel funds in Texas. *P.18, 22, 50, 150, 157, 162, 172*

Richard Sudek is an associate professor of entrepreneurism at Chapman University Graduate School of Business, is Director of the Leatherby Center for Entrepreneurism and Business Ethics, and Chairman Emeritus of the Tech Coast Angels, the largest angel group in the United States. *P.32*

Chapter One. STARTING UP!

Do you have that entrepreneurial DNA?
By Dave Berkus

My immediate family members were entrepreneurs from as far back as I can trace. Dad was a jeweler, then a furniture store owner. Mom wrote books and articles from her college days until she could no longer see the keyboard. One grandfather owned and maintained his apartment houses. The other was a grocer, then a jeweler.

So it seemed perfectly natural that my brother and I find our separate callings as entrepreneurs from the very start. I took pictures of neighbor children, developing them in my bedroom closet, selling the prints to those neighborhood families. I was twelve. The prints were not very good. At fifteen, I started a recording business that would pay my way through college, a business that I'd take public in a limited IPO years after, before getting into the computer software business in its infancy. My brother, who had an artist streak where no-one could identify its roots, drew pictures that were extraordinary, and became one of the world's one hundred most noted architects.

What drove my brother and me to perform, to risk so much, to skirt bankruptcy, to press on again and again? For us, I believe it was two important things.   First, our family DNA made us comfortable talking about risk and self-discovery in running a business, even without formal training. Second, and more importantly, my brother and I watched our dad run his business in the most conservative manner possible, refusing to expand or take risks, comfortable with a steady income and no prospects of building wealth through building business equity. Both of us reacted in different ways, but in common was the urge to take much more risk, to push the boundaries, to succeed spectacularly or fail and start again. We reacted to our view of dad's conservatism.

We tell the story that dad was offered the general store franchise in the brand new park in Anaheim soon to be built by Walt Disney. The price for the franchise in 1953 was $50,000. Dad turned it down, stating that there was no chance of success for a park so far from downtown Los Angeles. His two sons observed, and perhaps reacted in later years by pushing to take the chance for themselves equal to that declined by dad.

Are you a DNA-based entrepreneur? Or are you starting out to build the next Cisco Systems because you know how your employer has failed to do so? Or do you want freedom from the senseless bureaucracy you face daily in your present job? Have you found the cure for cancer and need to bring it to the world? Or is your reason for risk more basic – that you found an easy opportunity to fill a need and you have the skill and desire to take that chance.

Think for a minute about your real reasons for taking this ride. It will help you to make better decisions about future risk, about your tolerance for it, and about your inner-self.

The most important person on the startup team
By David S. Rose

Since Bill Hewlett joined with Dave Packard in 1939 to create what is today one of the world's largest computer companies, there has been an evergreen debate as to who is more important in starting a tech company: the techie or the business guy? Steve Jobs or Steve Wozniak? Bill Gates or Steve Ballmer? Jim Clark or Marc Andreessen?

I propose that it is time to reject the notion of the *business man* or *business woman* entirely. The underlying problem is that there are really three different components here, and like the classic three-legged school, they are all essential for success, albeit with differing relative economic values. What confuses us is that the components can all reside in one person, or multiple people. And what upsets people is that there are different quantities of those components available in the economic marketplace; and the law of supply and demand is pretty good about consequently assigning a value to them.

Perhaps surprisingly, the components are NOT the traditional coding/business pieces; nor are they even coding /user interface / business / sales, or whatever. Rather, here is the way I see it, from the perspective of a serial entrepreneur turned serial investor, listed in order of decreasing availability:

1) THE CONCEPT: A business starts with an idea, and while the idea may (and likely will) change over time; it has to be good at some basic level for it to be able to succeed in the long run. How excited am I likely to be when I see a plan for a new generation of buggy whip, or another me-too social network? The basic concept has to make some kind of sense given the technical, market and competitive environment, otherwise nothing else matters. BUT good ideas are NOT hard to find. There are millions of them out there. The key to making one of them into a home-run success brings us to:

2) EXECUTION SKILLS: It is into this one bucket that ALL of the 'traditional' pieces fall. This is where you find the superb Rails coder, *and* the world-class information architect, *and* the consummate sales guy, *and* the persuasive business development person, *and* the brilliant CFO. Each of the functions is crucial, and each is required to bring the good idea to fruition. In our fluid, capitalistic, free-market society, the marketplace is generally very efficient about assigning relative economic value to each of these functional roles, based upon both the direct result of their contribution to the enterprise and their scarcity (or lack thereof) in the job market.

That is why it is not uncommon to see big enterprise sales people making high six figure - or even seven figure - salaries or commissions, while a neophyte coder might be in the low five figure range. Similarly, a crackerjack CTO might be in the mid six figures, but a kid performing inside sales may start at the opposite end of the spectrum. Coding, design, production, sales, finance, operations, marketing, and the like are all execution skills; and without great execution, success will be very hard to come by.

But, as noted, each of these skills is available at a price, and given enough money it is clearly possible to assemble an all-star team in each of the above areas to execute any good idea. That, however, will not be enough. Why? Because it is missing the last, vital leg of the stool, and the one that ultimately–when success does come–will reap the lion's share of the benefits:

3) THE ENTREPRENEUR: Entrepreneurship is at the core of starting a company, whether tech-based or otherwise. It is *not* any one of the functional skills above, but rather the combination of vision, passion, leadership, commitment, communication skills, hypomania, fundability, and, above all, willingness to take risks, that brings together all of the forgoing pieces - and creates from them an enterprise that fills a value-producing role in our economy. And because it is *this* function which is the scarcest of all, it is *this* function that (adjusting for the cost of capital) ends up with the lion's share of the money from a successful venture.

It is crucial to note that the entrepreneurial function can be combined into the same package as a techie (Bill Gates), a sales guy (Mark Cuban), a user interface maven (Steve Jobs), or a financial guy (Michael Bloomberg). And that it is the critical piece which ultimately (if things work out) gets the big bucks.

The moral of the story is that, for a successful company, we need to bring together all of the above pieces, realize that whatever functional skill set the entrepreneur starts out with can be augmented with the others, and understand that the lion's share of the rewards will (after adjusting for the cost of capital), go to the entrepreneurial role, as has happened for hundreds of years.

Plans? Humbug! Show me what you're made of.
By David Steakley

Business plans are interesting. But, as a famous field marshal [1] said, no battle plan survives contact with the enemy. I have found it more important to assess the capabilities of the founding team to react, revise and pivot *(quickly change direction)*, than it is important to assess the business plan. How do you know whether your founder team and your added executives have the right stuff to survive contact with the enemy?

In addition to the ability to pivot, character matters, too. As my kids have commenced driving, I've harped incessantly, hopefully to the point of their nausea, on the notion that they should always have in mind that everyone driving on the road is in a massive conspiracy to collide with them, and make it appear that the collision was an accident. "Just assume everyone is trying to kill you," I say.

I take this approach to angel investing. I begin by assuming that the founders of the company are incompetent, psychopathic, lying con-men and thieves; and I try to convict them of these charges. I ask them innocuous questions, and try to check as many seemingly inconsequential details of their story as I can. Where did you go to school? When did you graduate? In what field was your degree? What was your first job? Why did you leave that job? Where did you grow up? Did you play sports in high school? What are your hobbies?

Faithful in little; faithful in much. If someone will deceive about a small matter, he will deceive about anything and everything. I don't do business with liars. If I am unsuccessful in proving these charges, then, perhaps the company is a candidate for investment.

I was a partner at a large global consulting firm. We hired literally hundreds of thousands of graduates every year. They had no meaningful experience. The only way to evaluate them was to look for a kind of raw, athletic talent. To help us in this, we adopted a technique which I believe is now universally used, but which was unusual at the time. We called it *behavioral interviewing.* This technique relies on identifying specific traits and characteristics which one wishes to find, either negatively or positively, and then asking the candidate to tell specific true stories about situations in which s/he would have had an opportunity to demonstrate the traits in question. A lot of the value of this technique relies on the interviewer being extremely aggressive with the candidate about the minutest of details within the story offered.

For the founders of companies in which I am considering investing, I have concluded that flexibility, intellectual nimbleness, and a relentless focus on dispassionate examination of factual evidence of results, are some relatively rare traits with which I cannot ignore. "Tell me about a time when you changed your mind about something important," I will ask. "Tell me about a time when what you were doing wasn't working. How did you know it wasn't working? What was the problem? What did you do?" "Tell me about a time when you screwed up big time. What happened? What did you do?" I will ask questions about the tiniest details of their stories. What were you wearing? What time of day was that?

I have actually had people respond along the lines of "I don't recall a time when I screwed up." Or "Sometimes I have been let down by my subordinates and my partners, though." Check, please!

But, a more common problem is that you find out by detailed questioning that the story presented is not really a true specific story, but a theoretical composite story, which reflects theoretical behavior the interviewee assumes you want to hear about. I don't want to work with these people. They are trying to tell me what I want to hear, and they do not want to admit the possibility of fault.

I want to work with people who are pleased to discover mistakes, errors, and opportunities for improvement. I will not work with people who hide mistakes, who ignore errors, and who pretend that everything is wonderful. I want to work with people who face the truth.

One of my very favorite entrepreneurs is the shining example of taking himself to task over errors and missteps, and of a constant vigilant search for how things are going wrong in his businesses. Recently he launched a unit which developed a casual browser-based online game, monetized through micro-transactions for virtual in-game goods. One of the beautiful things about this kind of business is the depth and immediacy of information available about performance and results. So, when something is changed, you find out immediately how the change affects results. This company has been through so many iterations of its model that I have lost track. I love the willingness to experiment, and the perpetual dissatisfaction with how things are going, and the relentless quest for improvement. This guy is going to make me a lot of money, or die trying.

So, focus on the personal traits and characteristics of your team. Things will definitely go wrong. You want to have some idea of how your team will react when that inevitably happens.

(1)   Helmuth Von Moltke the Elder, 1871

Project cash flow - not just profit - during start-up.
By Dave Berkus

Cash is everything to a new business. How many times do we have to say this? The days of being able to trust that there will be an investor or lender on the other end of a call or email whenever needed ended with the 2000 and 2008 bursts of those respective bubbles. It's entirely possible that Amazon could not be created and funded today with its planned seven years until profitability.

Early stage investors who take a chance on new businesses, often now plan their investments around the notion – or hope – that they can fund one or two rounds to lead the business to profitability. There is no longer a guarantee that VCs and later stage investors will be waiting at the run-out point of the angel money to pick up and grow the company.

Business plans that I see often show three to five years of projections, demonstrating profitability at the end of so many months of operation. Most every one of these uses an accrual basis for determining breakeven, never attempting to predict the cash impact of capital investment, slow collection times, large deposits upon leases, and other major items that consume cash.

Worse yet, most show rapid gains in revenues but do not account for the extra cash it takes for working capital to grow the business at the rate projected. If a business takes an average of sixty days to collect cash from the time it invests in the product with costs of inventory or labor, then shipping and billing, then the business will need increased working capital to pay its expenses including payroll while it waits for the cash to come in the door.

Recast your projections using cash, not accrual, as the measure for planning. An accrual statement is nice to produce. It confirms that the business is capable of ultimately throwing off positive cash flow. But only accurate projections of cash by the week or month as appropriate will assure the survival of a business in a rapid growth cycle, or even a startup raising just enough to make it to breakeven.

Big corporations are just slow to act.
By David Steakley

How do you judge a company's prospects, if a corporate business-to-business sale has to be your game? If your company's market is huge corporations, how do you convince investors you can crack the market, and how do you deliver?

To answer this, you have to understand the challenges of getting paperwork signed and checks issued, in a big company. You'll notice I didn't say "the challenges of selling," because this is seldom the crucial challenge. I am assuming that you have an awesome product or service which cleverly solves some tough problem and promises to deliver solid ROI for the buyer.

Just to be up front, as an investor, I am allergic to companies which rely on making potentially huge sales to corporate clients. The corporate B2B sales cycle produces a harshly binary outcome: either the company dies while waiting for a corporate client to sign the paperwork and remit the funds, or else it delivers gigantic outsized sales with relatively little effort.

I routinely see prospective investments which rely by their nature upon selling to corporate customers. I have learned through bitter experience that little can be predicted from analyzing the company's product or service. Of course, you'd think the company has to have a useful, valuable, or somewhat unusual product in order to be successful. But, from a standpoint of efficient analysis of the company's prospects, this is not the place to start.

Big corporations are just slow to act. The time needed for decision increases as a factor of the number of people involved in the decision process. The number of people involved in the decision process varies as a factor of the amount of money involved, the number of places in the company affected by the transaction, and the duration and contractual obligations of the commitment.

I have found that the predictor of success is really extremely simple: tell me the name, phone number, birthdate and favorite brand of scotch of the senior corporate executive who is going to be your first customer, and tell me how much he is going to pay you in the next twelve months. Now, I am not saying you have to sell only to scotch drinkers, but you get my point: the predictor is your intimate knowledge of people you already know who need your product, want your product, and who know and trust you to the point that they will work hard to overcome the obstacles of closing the deal.

In other words, you have to have inside agents. You have to know, find, create, recruit, whatever, senior corporate executives who will relentlessly and stubbornly perform the unnatural acts required to close the sale.

Occasionally, I have seen success with companies getting started by using channels, i.e., other companies which are already providing or selling some product or service to your customers, who will tuck your product or service into their bag of tricks in return for a slice of the revenue. But it is very, very difficult to get a new product started this way. Once you've established the product, and the channels can be persuaded that your product provides them with relatively easy incremental revenues; channels are a fantastic way to scale your sales effort without fixed costs.

The great advantage of the B2B market is the potentially huge size of revenues from just one sale. Those revenues tend to be very durable, as quite often, you are getting your offerings wired into the DNA of the customer.

Before you tackle the corporate market, be sure you understand the challenges of this market, and think carefully about your product design and your sales approach, to reduce the barriers to closing sales as much as possible.

Plan your exit even as you plan your debut.
By JJ Richa

This insight seems counter-intuitive to many entrepreneurs when starting their fresh, new business.

But when you start a new business, buy an existing business, or as you plan to grow your existing business, one very important aspect to consider is the need to think about your eventual exit. That decision, made at the very start of your effort, determines whether to take outside investor money, "bootstrap" or build it with personal resources only, or some combination.

Are you trying to establish a lifestyle business that generates income without plans to sell it in the future? Or are you building equity in a business that you may want to transform into cash? Depending on your goals, the type of business you choose and the way you grow it should be aligned with your end-game objectives.

Think of potential exit strategies:

- Going Public (IPO)
- Merger (Combine)
- Sale (Acquisition)
- Buyout (LBO, MBO)
- Succession (Family)
- Shutting Down (Asset Liquidation)

Regardless of your situation, it is important to start planning for the end game now. You need to prepare for that exit every step along the way. You'll need to build value and equity in your company by creating unique products, services, relationships and distribution channels, building an intellectual property portfolio and expanding your customer base.

Depending on your situation, an exit may be beneficial to you, your family, your employees, or your investors that helped you get started.

When it comes to your own benefits and the benefit to family and employees - consider all of the time, energy and money you put into your business. It only makes sense to know when and how you will see the rewards of your work. Where do you want to be down the road? How will your business planning and execution help get you there? When do you plan to retire? Without a clear plan to strategically leave your business, you risk never fulfilling both your personal and business goals.

Investors expect to see your ultimate goal to include an exit strategy - at least for them. For the most part, having an exit strategy is one of the ways investors assess the business' potential for success, and often the only way they would consider making an investment to guarantee an acceptable return on their money.

So what are my possible exit options?

Going Public: You can sell your company via the stock market in an initial public offering or IPO. An IPO allows investors to easily liquidate their investment and is a highly attractive exit strategy if the plan can demonstrate growth to a large enough company to warrant an IPO exit. The good news is that you stand the chance to get the biggest dollar payout of any other exit strategy. The bad news is that it is very expensive to manage an IPO, and you can easily spend up to millions of dollars on attorneys, accountants, and other fees. In addition, there are a lot of restrictions to achieving liquidity through an IPO. If your business is outside of the tech sector and has less than $50 million in revenues, generally you should consider a different strategy.

Merger: A merger is defined as two companies getting together, establishing a value for each company, and then combining the two to form one bigger company. In most mergers, the company shareholders receive stock in the larger pre-merger company which is presumably worth more than the stock held in each independent company. Therefore, be aware that in a merger, you may not actually receive cash for some time, certainly not during the merger itself. There are many times where having the resources of both companies creates a more valuable entity. However, mergers usually result in less control for the smaller entity, as you cede some power to the bigger company's management.

Sale: Selling your company is the most common exit strategy for business owners – to someone else or to some other company. For the most part it entails a transaction that can be conducted between two private parties without all the government regulations and oversight that occurs with an IPO unless you are selling to a public company. A sale typically results in the seller of the company receiving cash in exchange for the company shares or assets. The tricky part of any sale is valuing the company. Since most small businesses are privately held, the ultimate transaction price in a sale is sometimes more art than science. Make sure you get more than one appraisal of the business so that you have confidence that the price is right. This exit option allows you to completely sever your ties with your business, unless you and the buyer agree to equity in the acquiring company as part of your proceeds, which usually occurs as part of a transition period to keep the seller on board for a period of time to guarantee a smooth transition.

Buyout: Buyouts come in many flavors including Management Buyout (MBO) and leveraged buyout (LBO) to name a few. If another company comes in and takes over your business, you're being bought-out.

Typically, the buyer would be another company or individual with experience in the same line of work and who will take over your business on the basis of buying out your ownership. These transactions are often tied to the business performance at the time of the buyout and shortly after you leave. Sellers usually hope that the acquiring company pays the entire purchase price upfront. Buyers want some or much or the purchase price to be dependent upon continued performance of the company.

Another way of paying for the business could be based on what is known as a Leveraged Buyout (LBO), where the buyer leverages the future cash of the business to pay off their debt to you assumed as part of the purchase price. In other words, the assets of your company are used to borrow against in order to pay for the purchase, adding debt to the company after the sale, and increasing its interest expense and risk of ultimate survival.

A Management Buyout (MBO) is when managers and/or employees buy out your interests in the business. Just like another company buying out the business, the management buyout can be arranged either with a cash option, an LBO, or a combination of both. An important advantage of the MBO is that the buyers have been and will continue to be familiar with the business, customers, employees and vendors, thereby making for a smoother transition.

Succession: Keeping the business in the family could be attractive if you have willing and able family members. Keys to a successful family succession include properly preparing both the family member as well as the business for the transition. Family succession must be planed years in advance with ample of time reserved for training your future owners. In order to provide as much training as possible, individuals involved in the succession should be given tasks and responsibilities in all of the business aspects of the company rotating between all departments so that experience and knowledge can be gained across all major business activities. Common challenges associated with this option include potential family tensions, decisions made with emotion rather than reason, tax implications, and the possibility that you may not be able to cash out if part of the purchase price is in the form of a promissory note dependent upon the profits of the ongoing business.

Shutting Down: You can gain some amount of liquidity by shutting down the business and selling the assets (in asset liquidation). The major challenge is to be able to find buyers who feel that the business assets have value, and for you to be able to negotiate a fair price for those assets, some of them intangible and difficult to value. With this kind of exit strategy, you would usually be getting the smallest amount of money because you are selling the raw assets and finding intangible assets such as customer list worth almost nothing.

Although this option may seem to be the easiest because it requires little negotiation and no transfer of control, it can be the most emotional. When you close your business, there can be feelings of loss and little financial reward. However, this option may be the most reasonable if your business is highly dependent on you, if you are faced with an unexpected change in health, or if the economy or other circumstances make it impractical to seek out an alternative exit. Your business's legal structure will influence how to close down with the least amount of financial and legal implications. Sole proprietorships can simply cease operations and pay off any outstanding liabilities. However, there are other conditions to consider if you are operating as a partnership, a limited liability company or a corporation.

Regardless of your exit strategy, it is imperative that you have the right team of advisors on your side to guide you through the process. These include accountants, attorneys, investment bankers, or others who are experienced and have "seen the movie before." Except for shutting down your business and liquidating its assets, valuation of your business becomes the most important aspect when it comes to an exit. It is highly recommended to have all your finances and accounting in order and hire qualified valuation professionals to assist you in this process.

Accurate assumptions lead to defendable plans.
By Dave Berkus

The biggest error in planning may not be spreadsheet calculation error. Or cost estimation. It is most often missed assumptions about the market, the competition, the speed of adoption, or other critical metrics you've researched, or selected, or even just guessed at to create your plan.

Where did you get the data to drive your assumptions of market size or market share? Most entrepreneurs quote a resource for market size, but fail to then take the next step to eliminate all parts of that market unreachable by the company or product. For example, if you supply software to the chip design industry, do you segment your market into digital and analog users, into high end or inexpensive buyers, and into which languages or platforms users demand or request?

It's easy to find someone to quote a size of market estimate. I became something of my industry's source for such a number when I carefully catalogued the 160 players both domestic and international, estimated revenues from knowing the number of employees or installations for each (which were often public knowledge or stated by those companies.) I then created a gross domestic and gross international annual market size estimate for my industry's products. No-one challenged this number, and it became an unattributed source of the metric for market size for years. Perhaps there was no other way to project the size of that market. But many decisions were made within my company walls, and surely by competitors, based upon those numbers.

Then there is the famous entrepreneur's statement about market share: "All I need to sell is one percent of the total available market to make this a rampant success." We call that the "gloves in China" syndrome when analyzing assumptions within business plans. Without a trace of how the business will get that one percent, the entrepreneur confidently shows that this is all it takes to make us all rich. Even if the total number of annual units in a market is known, the leap to a percent of that market without a specific plan is often a fatal one.

And these are just two of the many assumptions that underlie any business plan. At the very least, all assumptions should be driven by numbers separately listed in an "assumptions section" of the planning spreadsheet, allowing the reader to manipulate those assumptions to see the various outcomes, and challenge the numbers for the benefit of all who have to defend them.

Include your labor value in your plan.
By Dave Berkus

Investors love it when entrepreneurs draw little or no money from their startups. It extends the cash available for research and other necessary fixed costs and gives the fragile, young company more "runway" to get to breakeven.

But when forecasting the ultimate viability of a business, many times an entrepreneurial founder uses a low, unsustainable salary rate for him or herself in order to show early breakeven. And that is the quandary for investors. If you had to replace yourself with a professional hired to duplicate your skills, what would you have to pay in salary and incentive today? That amount is almost always higher, much higher, than the amount budgeted for the entrepreneur.

You could start by charging more for your executive salary, then paying out less in cash, accruing the rest into a payable amount due to the entrepreneur. But that is a messy way to demonstrate that you are taking less than market wages from your company. Ultimately, the accrued difference will amount to a large enough liability that several things could happen, all of them negative.

The IRS could see that you are not paying yourself interest on the accrued debt, and consider it invested capital, eliminating your ability to repay yourself in the future. Worse yet, the IRS would then consider the accrued amount to be taxable income upon which no tax was paid, since the accrued labor as an investment has value that was not accounted for from previously taxed earnings. Or you could voluntarily convert the loan into stock with a single journal entry and a stock certificate. But the tax effect would be the same if audited – you would owe tax on the booked value.

The solution is to explain to potential investors that you are projecting under-market wages for the founder(s) for a period of time, perhaps until breakeven, and then to agree with them that you will move to market rate at that time.

My dad said: "Never take on a business partner."

By Dave Berkus

My dad was a smart businessman, even if not formally trained. He occasionally gave me advice that turned out to be more than wise, looking back at subsequent experience and events. His personal teaching event was a typical experience, as I reflect now upon the tens of partnerships I have counseled over the years. Most often, one partner remained active as another partner drifted away from the business, no longer carrying the weight anticipated at start-up.

It's just one – the most prevalent – of the many things that can happen to well-meaning partners after time changes plans, and after the business passes through phases of growth or contraction.

I recall one very personal situation when I was very young, that reinforces Dad's advice. Through my college years, I managed a phonograph record production and manufacturing business that I created as a senior in high school, using independent contractors in local venues to record and edit the original tapes from recording musicals and performances from schools, colleges, churches and organizations throughout the USA and Canada - and then to sell the records to the appropriate audiences.

It grew to significant size during my college years, and I associated myself with a "strategic partner" throughout those years, ceding to him all recording and editing of work throughout the large home territory, and any national jobs we received. The agreement was that he would retain all of the revenues generated from those activities. We called ourselves "partners" and received lots of press, even nationally, as we managed our teenage business.

A year after graduation from college, I left for six months to serve my active duty obligation in the US Navy, while others took care of accounting and customer relations. And my "partner" left the company without notice and set up a competing company in my absence, never saying a word to any of us. I was bitter, but unable to do anything about it, since there was no partnership agreement. Luckily, after my return from active duty, my company flourished and his remained a small, one person operation for the rest of its existence. But, as they say, everything he learned, he learned from me. Dad was right, even if I learned the lesson years later.

So pay attention to the next insight, authored by JJ Richa, in which our guest author addresses the issue with a checklist of "how to" items that will help assure a successful partnership...

The five C's of Business Partners: a marriage without the sex

By Richard Sudek

In working with entrepreneurs over the years, I have learned that the difference between success and failure is often centered on the people aspects of the business rather than strategy, finance, or operations. It is not that strategy, finance, and operations are not important, but rather failure of the business is more likely attributed to people issues. Nowhere is this more evident than with the issues related to business partners. Thinking about a business partnership like a marriage might be helpful in how you go about selecting a business partner.

You are likely to spend more time with your business partner than your spouse in the early stages of launching a business. This relationship may last 5-20 years. In many ways having a business partner is like getting married. You will spend a lot of time with that person (many years), you are likely to have employees (similar to having kids), you are likely to have arguments (but no make-up sex), you are likely to compromise (will not always win each fight), and the breakup can be messy and expensive (divorce court). When you look at it this way, you may want to spend some extra time considering how to select a business partner. Thus, when thinking about partnerships I suggest you think of the 5 C's: *Confidence, Competency, Complementary, Compatibility*, and

Contract. Let's start with confidence, since this is about you rather than your partner.

Confidence is the first "C" because it refers to the confidence you have to launch your business. Sometimes an entrepreneur picks a partner because they experience some insecurity. This can range from emotional immaturity to functional insecurity. For instance, a good friend who now is in his 60s and was a very successful entrepreneur said he picked his first partner because he was insecure about his knowledge of finance. He felt he needed someone to compensate for this. It turned out that he really only needed a good bookkeeper and CPA. This partnership did not work well since the partner did not have much else to offer.

This might be the toughest "C" for younger entrepreneurs to deal with since it is really about self-assessment and introspection. How well do you really know yourself? Know your limitations? Your strengths? Ability to admit your weaknesses? You need to ask the question: Why do I need a partner? Is this what the business really needs? Or is this what I need? If what you need and the business needs are not the same, you might be seeking a partner for the wrong reason. Seek advice from mentors and other entrepreneurs who have been down this path before.

Competency is related to assessing a potential partner. The more experience you have the more you learn how to assess competency in others. This can range from a functional area such as marketing, or a people attribute like trust. Again, many younger entrepreneurs simply do not have the experience to do this well. This is when asking for help is important. The same entrepreneur who picked the wrong partner in the previous paragraph said now he would have multiple people interview a potential person, perform more due diligence on their background, and be much more thorough. When he was younger, he had too much arrogance to ask for help. The older you get, the less you worry about what you know, and focus more on what is the best way to get what you need.

Complementary is for picking a partner with complementary skills. Most of us think of this in functional areas, however, this is not the only area to seek complementary skills. It is important not to have significant overlap. For instance, if you are good at marketing, don't select a partner with a good marketing background. Find someone with technology, operations, manufacturing, or finance experience. Ask yourself, what skill does the business absolutely need?

But more importantly, are you complementary enough with this person to help make a complete CEO? Some of us act quickly and don't think deeply. Some act slowly but think deeply. Some of us are more enthusiastic, or volatile, or quiet. The worst thing you can do is find someone similar in personality and functional areas. Two technologists who are introverted are unlikely to make a good partnership. Steve Jobs and Steve Wozniak were a great example of being very different, yet these differences made for a very effective partnership.

Compatibility is related to how similar partners are on the dimensions of work ethic, integrity, style, and eventual outcome of the business or the exit among other issues. This is more of a personal fit issue rather than a functional fit. In other words - are you both going to work 100 hours a week in the beginning? When one partner feels they are putting more effort into the business, it is likely that resentment will build over time. Is how you frame integrity - and how you view different difficult choices that involve ethical issues similar? Something as simple as how to lay-off an employee and how much severance to offer can create significant disconnect with partners.

One time I was brought in to coach two partners. They had raised over a half million dollars, had fifteen employees, and thought they had strategic planning issues. What they had was a relationship problem. I ended up doing more couples counseling than CEO coaching or strategy work. They had never had the "exit" talk. They had not decided how or when they were going to exit, and what their personal dollar goal was for an exit. Be sure your personal issues related to the business have been discussed and are compatible.

Contract is the last "C" and might seem the most obvious. Every partnership needs to have a partner agreement, or in marriage terms, a pre-nup. Do you know exactly how you are going to part ways if things do not go as you plan, or if you simply want to get out? Do you know how you are going to value the company, how long it will take to pay the amount, and what the penalties are if you are late in paying? Worse yet, what if your partner dies and you are stuck (both legally and emotionally) with the remaining spouse who does not know anything about the business or industry? Marriage is till death-do-you-part, but business partnerships include what happens after death. The problem with this level of detail is that it can be an uncomfortable discussion for most. Consider hiring a third party to walk you through this. Since that person should not have ulterior motives, as is more likely to ask the very difficult questions about what might appear to be an unlikely scenario questions.

Selecting a partner is sometimes necessary, and extremely difficult. Few of us are complete CEOs. So spend the time and energy to make the best decision you can. Ask for help to assess potential partners and to dig into personal values and issues. And *always* have a contract.

Editor's note: After reading Richard Sudek's Five C's above, here is a detailed checklist from JJ Richa to use in creating and managing a successful partnership. - DWB

How to make a business partnership a success
By JJ Richa

Business partnerships have their advantages and disadvantages. Taking on a business partner is like a entering into a marriage. In general, partnerships are easy to get into and difficult to get out of. Certain guidelines should be taken into consideration along with a path to follow – from dating to pre-nup to marriage – all of which can be applied to a business partnership.

Taking on a business partner can be an excellent strategic decision in helping move the business forward. It should be well thought out for all parties involved. The relationship needs to be synergistic financially, emotionally, and operationally. All parties need to perform due diligence to ensure that the assumptions are correct, that neither partner has financial issues which could affect the partnership, and that the opposite partner has the skills to contribute to the partnership.

Most of the important benefits for partnering include:

- Combining of complimentary skill sets
- Access to new markets
- Addition of new services or product lines
- Addition of essential expertise and knowledge to propel the business forward
- Open doors to new distribution channels
- Access to new technologies
- Access to capital unavailable to either partner singly

Certain steps should be taken before entering into a partnership.

1. Personal assessment and getting to know one another:

   - Work together on 2-3 projects before an agreement is consummated
   - Determine the commitment of the potential partners. Is the potential partner in for the long haul?
   - Identify each of the partner's unique contribution. Does the potential partner bring specialized knowledge, skills, leadership, or experience that compliments others?
   - Understand each person's personal goals. Are each set of goals consistent with the other's including for example personal wealth, business success, and autonomy?
   - Determine trust and Values. Is there trust between the parties? Do the proposed partners share a set of common values? Core values are none negotiable. Be ready to walk away when others are willing to negotiate their own values or try to negotiate others.

2. Determine personal and business goals:

- Contribution: What will the new partner contribute? Example: cash, assets, equipment, connections... Regardless of what it is, a partner's contribution needs to increase the value of the business.
- Compensation: What are compensation expectations? Example: salary, equity, joint venture, etc... Can the business afford it?
- Control: What type of control is the new partner looking for? Example: percent   of   ownership,   officer/operational, director/board member... What are the parties willing to give up in return for the prospect of business success?
- Brand and Success: Is the new partner dedicated to ensuring brand continuity and contribute to the success, or just to ride on what has been established by the other?

3. Create roles and guidelines in the potential partnership:

- What role and responsibility will each of the partners have including operation, financial, sales, marketing, etc..?
- How will decisions be made and by whom? Is it by committee?
- Will each have certain level of decision making authority? Will the new process impair quick decision making?
- Will authority limits be defined, and processes and procedures put in place?
- What is the understanding if one of the partners wants out or wants more? What is the understanding if things go downhill/uphill?

4. Perform preliminary due diligence:

- Review the business plan including marketing, sales strategies and financial needs
- Review long term company debt, goals, objectives and financial projections
- Review financial statements – up to 3 years if available
- Review tax returns - up to 3 years if available
- Research and talk to existing and past customers

5. Create partnership agreement basic terms:

- Define Key Performance Indicators (KPIs.) How will the success of the business be measured?
- Clarify decision making and dispute resolution processes
- Define each partner's title and position
- Define management responsibilities and job descriptions
- Detail authority limits for each partner
- Clarify operation responsibilities and metrics used to measure performance
- Define vacations and time off policies such as with partners vacationing at the same time
- Determine compensation for each partner
- Exit strategy planning, including determining what happens when one partner leaves, if closing the business, if selling the business, creating a mutual buy/sell agreement, and more.

Depending on the legal structure of the business, different types of formal agreements may be required.

Partnership agreement should never be 50/50 regardless of the perception of compatibility at the time of execution. There must be some method of resolving a tie that is predetermined in the agreement.

Potential partners should follow and apply these guidelines independently. This should be followed by a joint meeting to determine commonalities, synergies, and conflicts. If necessary, this is the time to bring in an impartial third party to facilitate any possible conflicts and resolutions.

It is highly recommended that legal document are created and/or reviewed by a business transaction attorney. All agreements should be in writing and signed by all parties involved. Regardless of what method is taken to reach an agreement among partners, avoid some of the common mistakes. These include premature rejection of ideas by the other partner, prematurely judging others, one-sided financial consideration, and not sticking to core values.

Build a company - not just a product.
By Dave Berkus

Some businesses are built around a single idea. And sometimes that idea is just too small a slice of the big picture to be interesting to investors. There was a recent investor event where I was keynote speaker, on stage only after several panels of experts had wowed the audience with their predictions and observations. One of the panelists made a point that resonated with me.

She stated that she had rejected the investment being discussed, because in her mind the entire company was "just a button, on a feature, in an app." That comment sent me thinking about relevance, about longevity, and about market size for some of these entrepreneurial applicants looking for funding.

If you have invented a game that will be marketed as a new app in the app store, have you created enough of a model to create an ongoing company, or just another app that will compete with the hundreds of thousands already in the store? Is your game using a unique engine, or series of animated characters, or method of play that will break ground with potential players, inducing them to look to you for more and more unique games over time?

Far too many companies have been created around a button on a feature, and not upon a solution to a need in answer to a void in the market. Investors have seen this game before. We match what we see to what has succeeded for us in the past. And rarely do we see a plan for a single product that is not part of a larger vision, and remain interested long enough to ask for more information.

There are exceptions. The famously popular app, "Draw It," might at first seem an exception, until you dig deeper to find a dense plan around a series of social engagement products planned to follow. Can you extend your product into a planned series? Plan to create apps, not buttons, and not features.

Ready, aim, fire. Really?

By Dave Berkus

You've surely heard the variations on this theme. "Ready, fire aim" was popular in the 1990's, accredited to any of several authors. I used the term to describe my efforts in the artificial intelligence field, experimenting with new devices, the lisp programming language, and our first trial installations. It seemed an ideal way to describe a scrappy, entrepreneurial activity.

So why do so many business-book authors stress the opposite behavior? Ready, FIRE, aim. What happens to careful planning, sure-fire metrics, quality test scenarios, market research, a good business plan – all in place before pulling the trigger of a new opportunity.

And who is right here?

If you're seeking investment from anyone other than friends and family, you're probably going to have to navigate through the exercise of careful planning, documentation and execution. Investors are a fickle bunch in general. They want to know that their money is not just being thrown at an idea that will become a trial by fire – literally.

On the other side of the argument is the truth of the claim that numerous iterations in the form of rapid prototypes and execution of new ideas in the field quickly refine the product or service to meet the needs of the customer, and at a far faster and cheaper pace than with careful pre-planning.

In the software arena, there is a term for this: "cowboy coding." Without the need to carefully document the architecture and elements of a proposed application, a single programmer can much more quickly just code, test, and create revised code. Without even pausing to document the process internally, no-one can easily take over the job, if for any reason the cowboy coder is no longer in control. And the result? Typically, we call that "spaghetti code" to signify code that is so often changed that it no longer looks clean and traceable.

The conclusion is that the best process depends upon the product, its critical core nature to the business using it, and the way in which the entrepreneur approaches the need for outside investors.

Critical components of any operation or business must be carefully constructed, tested and inserted into the operation of the business. On the other hand, if a new free iPad app has bugs, they can be corrected in the next automatic update, and probably without much customer noise.

Which is better for you: rapid iteration or careful planning? What is your case for defending your method of creating new products or services?

The three step dance
By Dave Berkus

Creating a new company in a relative vacuum is an exercise in complete trust that the entrepreneur knows what's best for the customer, perhaps even without interaction with such a customer. It's probably happened, but not often enough to trust this method as a formula for success.

So, I've developed *the three step dance* in order to help form a repeatable method of how to create a great company from an early idea.

The first step: *Involve potential customers early*. Even if you know it all - wouldn't it be an excellent plan to try your idea out on enough actual or potential customers to measure reasonable feedback?

You can use or discard the information you receive. We now know that Steve Jobs created in relative secrecy several of his products that became massive industry drivers of change. The iPad probably would have failed before production, had he used feedback and research from past failures of tablets in any previous form as a guide. On the other hand, most products or services are created in response to a real or perceived need. And most of us are not Steve Jobs.

The second step: *Take feedback seriously.* Making the effort to gather metrics from the field in any form and then ignoring it, takes guts and determination - and in most cases a measure of stupidity. As I analyze business plans, I usually ask the entrepreneur early in the process whether s/he has tried this idea or prototype or mockup out on potential users. And if so, what was the response? And from how many people? In what related universe? I want to know that potential paying customers have been queried using enough information or a good enough model to get a real response worth taking seriously. Without this, any information received is suspect. And failure to make use of the information is a red flag for investors.

The third step: *Reiterate and return to customers for comments.* Seeking, then analyzing responses allows you to make changes to the plan and product in response. But what if the changes create other problems for the customer, or miss the mark, or don't drive these same customers to more positive responses? The best possible second round feedback should come from the very same people who took the time to review the offering the first time. They have context and should see effort and progress. Their comments should therefore be more valued than those from first-time respondents.

The three step dance:

1. Involve your customers early.
2. Take feedback seriously.
3. Reiterate and return to customers for comments.

So, why not design your product using your real and potential customers as consultants?

Eyeballs aren't everything.

By Dave Berkus

Back when we were all trying to figure out the real value of traffic on the web, we investors - and acquiring companies - got a bit crazy with metrics used to value acquisitions and investments. Since in most cases, there was no revenue in many of these companies, all trying to gain market share at any cost, we had to invent the metric to use. And the most logical one seemed to be "eyeballs" or number of unique users finding their way to the site or registering for the service.

And the numbers were staggering. Microsoft paid $9.00 per registered user for Hotmail. AOL paid $40.00 per registered user of ICQ, the early messaging service. I was the original investor and helped to grow GameSpy Industries, attracted to the fledgling company because of its million users each month, even though at the time there was no monetization to the traffic.

But, when the bubble burst in 2000, most of us quickly grew up. Revenue models became more important a measure than traffic, although market share was and still is an over-weighted part of the value of any Internet-based entity.

That is the quandary which entrepreneurs face today in building models for new companies around a web presence. Great revenue projections from a small user base lead to worries over sustainability. Low revenue projections but demonstrated (or projected) impressive numbers of unique users lead investors to think that there may be a future method of monetizing the user base that makes the company attractive, even while currently losing money.

I am an investor and advisor to one such company. Gaining users at a rate of 50% a month, the company has yet to find a revenue model that will pay for the increased costs of infrastructure needed to support the growth, let alone the fixed cost of operating the enterprise. And yet, users rave about the service, and spend long durations of time on the site.

Once we had what we thought was the answer, in allowing for display advertising on these sites. But the competition among sites has overwhelmed available inventory of paying advertisers, greatly reducing the cost per thousand views, and making display ads no longer a preferred revenue source for marginal sites.

We experimented with subscription-based charges for game sites and other sites supplying what we thought were indispensable services. In every case, those subscription models failed, as users found free alternatives. One of my companies had four million free beta gamers registered on the site, but lost all but 10,000 when attempting to charge $9.95 a month for a subscription.

What is the answer? New forms of advertising have been created to force user views, including pop-ups, pre-roll ads containing video content, and click-through display ads before allowing content views. Major newspapers and magazines, trying to reinvent themselves, are using the subscription model, as well as all of the above methods in their attempt to become relevant to a new and growing mobile and Internet-focused user base, with varying - but not too satisfying results.

Micropayments, in which services and information are delivered for pennies, requires an infrastructure for collecting, accumulating and billing that is still being experimented with, but showing promising results.

Giants like Facebook and Google have such large eyeball numbers that they can use display and positioning ads to achieve great profits. Most of us are still searching for the combination of monetization devices that work best for us. Free sites without monetization will disappear over time, and we will lose services we take for granted today. It is in the best interest of both Internet users *and* providers to find an acceptable way to charge for valuable services or information.

It's mostly in the execution.
By Dave Berkus

"Everybody's got a plan - until they are punched in the face," stated boxer Mike Tyson. My experience personally reviewing over three hundred executive summaries each year, all sent to me unsolicited, seems to bear out the truth in Tyson's statement. Anyone can build a good – or great – plan. Investors have to look behind the plan and at the entrepreneur and his or her team, knowing that, over time, most of us have come to the conclusion that it is the execution of the ever-changing plan, not the plan itself that makes a company a success.

Tyson's statement also addresses change. The 'punch in the face' is analogous to dealing with the business plan when it intersects with the realities of the market. Wham! I can't recall any of my companies hanging onto its original plan after some level of consumer feedback.

We built one of our companies upon forecasted metrics for a specific class of retail consumer base, but found that there wasn't enough money in our universe to pay for marketing to create that much dedicated traffic to our site. So we switched to distribution through partners which already had massive amounts of traffic, and concentrated in providing great content and great offers that more than made up for the sharing of revenues.

There is a name for such a change in focus, in this case from retail to wholesale. We call it a "pivot," a term now used to describe great management dealing with successfully refocusing a company in a new direction.

And most of us who invest in so many companies have come to the conclusion that our greatest profits over time come from investments in great management, groups that we are confident are able to execute even on average plans. Some label this as "Bet on the jockey, not the horse."

Burn the bridges behind.
By Frank Peters

I became an entrepreneur because I had to. My life in Corporate America wasn't going so well. I never got fired, but I did quit one job the day before I was to be let go. I used my employee discount that last day to purchase a Compaq luggable computer and drove with my brother to Las Vegas. Now, this would be questionable therapy for anyone who just became unemployed, except we were heading to *Comdex*, the annual computer show that would eventually grow huge as would the industry itself. I consider this trip the anniversary of the company's starting up, and made the trip 11 years in a row.

How was striking out on my own? I'd often say: "I created the company so no one could fire me." I never took a business course, never wrote a business plan, and never raised any outside capital.

As I look back at insights I might share, I wade through the trite suggestions of 'work hard' and 'treat the customer well.' But there's more. *Burn the bridges behind* comes to mind. I had no alternatives to success. I was not going back to corporate America. It wasn't a fall- back position. I had to be successful at my new software company. And it wasn't easy.

I remember taking a walk with my wife one evening and sharing my concerns over cash flow. My sales tax payments were due in the next few days, and I didn't have the money. Default would bring many consequences. But I did have an appointment, a sales opportunity the next morning. I woke up that next morning with a jolt - literally. An earthquake struck Los Angeles. In an hour I received a phone call from the friend who was in the office where I was due later that morning. He had made the introduction for my appointment. "People are pretty shook up here today. Some were stuck in an elevator. I don't know if today's the best day to come up." He wasn't telling me I couldn't come, so, because I had to, I did. I made the sale, and paid my debts. I always remember that 'back against the wall' feeling. It was stressful and yet so typical when running a small company.

This morning over coffee, my wife told me of a dream she had last night. It was about the earliest days of our life together when we moved to Westwood so I could attend UCLA. "Moving out west away from our families was one of the best things that could've happened to us at that early age," she recalled wistfully. "We had to make a go of it." It brought back the memories of landing at LAX in 1974 with three suitcases and $1,900 to our names. Like my eventual experience as an entrepreneur, we had to persevere. We had no alternatives. *We had burned our bridges behind.*

How many innovations are carefully planned?
By Dave Berkus

Most innovations come from responding to a customer's needs, or finding a niche where products need improvement or extension. It is rare to innovate using a blank sheet of paper in a room with bare walls and no other contributors.

Imagine the room in which several graduate business school student groups have gathered, tasked with coming up with an idea for a business plan competition. The group starts with a blank sheet, and toils through idea after idea, trying to come up with a product or service that might become the next FedEx. That is tough work, and not a very productive way to start a process. Sometimes, the result is spectacular. Most of the time, this form of thinking produces a plan that requires real work to imagine success.

I'd advise the students to do it differently. I'd advise them to pick a growing industry. Then find a short list of users, customers, and consultants in that industry who are known to be advanced in their thinking as demonstrated by their prior work. Then I'd advise them to visit the CEO. And ask, "What is it that bothers you most about your operation?" "What is you biggest problem, other than working capital?" "Where's your bottleneck in production or sales or development?" "If you could invent a solution, what would it be?"

Now that's how to find pain in an industry. And yet, few think to use this form of investigation. Yes, you can argue that probably Fred Smith might not have thought of FedEx if he had just interviewed rail or postal customers. But maybe someone would have given Smith the bare idea from which he could imagine a much bigger opportunity.

If you're starting a new company because you have a better way to do something, create something or market something, you have a head start. But if you're trying to think of what you want to produce, start with finding the pain in the marketplace, and set out to remove it.

Henry Ford famously said, "If I asked my customers what they wanted, they would have said 'a faster horse.'" As a mechanical genius, even that comment might have led Ford to envision a way to provide reliable, fast, inexpensive, mechanical horsepower. It is the process of leaping from a need to an eloquent solution that creates demand and ultimately success in the marketplace.

Chapter Two. RAISING MONEY

You may be at the stage where money is the lever you need to move your business to the next level. In this chapter, we will examine many forms that raising money can take, and analyze the relative benefits and problems with each.

You may be about to trade freedom for some new responsibilities – whether to a lender or to an investor.

And we'll examine some rules, best practices, and aids to success that you should know when raising money. Even if you are not at a point where you are looking for outside funds, this chapter will help you to understand many options, some of them relatively new, available to businesses of all sizes from start-up to mature.

The "inciting incident:" Movie scripts tell us how and when to look for investment.

By David Steakley

If you are a screenplay writer, you are familiar with the dogma of the inciting incident. In a movie, the inciting incident is the event at the beginning of the story which causes the hero's life to be completely transformed and irrevocably changed, and which makes the whole story unfold. Companies also need an inciting incident, because, more often than not, you often will depend upon selling your story to someone. What is the inciting incident for your company? How can you get to it more quickly and with less capital?

Every good story has an inciting incident. You may not spot it at first. For example, ask yourself: "What is the inciting incident in *The Godfather?*" This one is tricky, because it doesn't occur until 45 minutes into the film, when Vito Corleone is gunned down in the street. This event totally changes the life of Michael Corleone and makes the rest of the story happen. Ok, now you're an expert: quick, what's the inciting incident in *Star Wars?*

The terminology is from the movie industry, but the concept applies to all stories. Every good story has an inciting incident. I am father of four kids, tween to teens, and I sometimes kid them, as a seemingly pointless anecdote trickles to an end, with the capper "...and then you found five dollars?" This is amusing (to me, at least) because it points out that the story lacks an inciting incident.

Story seems to be an artifact of the human brain, and soul. It is a key part of what makes us human. Stories are the most important repository of wisdom, experience, knowledge, and learning. Story telling is often a key aspect of a great leader's talent. For example, while Steve Jobs was abusive, rude, and unappreciative, he had what his colleagues referred to a reality distortion field. He told his team how it was going to be, and even though his story of what was going to happen seemed to be completely unrealistic fantasy, he made his team believe the story, and his teams of believers made it come true.

I found myself explaining all this recently to a company team that was pitching me on its story. The company is building a website to match commercial tenants with commercial landlords. They told me all about why this is such a good idea: hard to manage price discovery in the commercial real estate market; fragmented information about vacancies obtained from landlords and brokers; and the large scale of transactions. They told me about their expertise and their network of contacts, and their early customers, and the promising results so far. They wanted to come to pitch to my angel network.

I told them they lacked an inciting incident. None of the angels in my group is likely to write a check without hearing and believing a story about how something dramatic is about to happen. The very best thing, I told them, would be to come back when the inciting incident has just happened, but the consequences have just begun to unfold. We talked about what this could be: major PR to drive tenants to the site; signing a deal with a major landlord to greatly increase listings; a scheme to source listings at massive scale from public data--there are a lot of possibilities, but they didn't have that element.

When you're selling your company to potential investors, you have to work hard on your story, and the story doesn't really begin until the inciting incident.

Answer: In Star Wars, the inciting incident is Darth Vader's attack on Princess Leia's spaceship.

Three things you need to have when raising money.
By Dave Berkus

Here's more advice from professional investors for aspiring entrepreneurs. Each of us has a list of things we look for early on when identifying whether we want to go to the next step in analyzing a plan. Come to think of it, these are good for challenging any business plan.

First: You must address *a big market,* large enough to allow a new entrant to have a shot at making a dent with a great product or service, and growing to a size that will make the company valuable at the exit. We often draw the line at believing that a company can capture enough of the market to generate over $40 million in revenues by the fifth year in the market. Many, many businesses will never be able to obtain this kind of market size or share. And often, these are the ones that will be bypassed by most organized angel groups when considering funding. Your big market can come from having a dominant share or just by being in a very large space. Both work - with the dominant share being preferred.

Second, you must have and be able to tell *an easy to understand story* to your prospective customers, suppliers and investors. If your product is too complex to describe in a few words, your opportunity to sell it will suffer, and investors will quickly lose interest or the ability to follow your explanation. I've often repeated that entrepreneurs must construct a short, single sentence "mantra" that explains what you do in as few words as possible, sometimes using the name of a well-known company as a proxy for your activities. "We are the Skype of Internet one-to many interactive broadcasting."

And third, you must have some *"secret sauce"* that is unique, and makes you and your offering stand out among the thousands of possible competitors. What gives you a head start, a barrier to entry, an extra value that others cannot easily emulate? Secret sauce is important to investors and to you in competing against a company with more money, a brand name, or a head start.

A big market. An easy-to-understand story. Secret sauce. Why not spend a few minutes right now, and explain to yourself how you address each.

Back to basics: List the forms of capital available.
By Dave Berkus

There are a number of options available to finance your startup or existing business. These options may or may not work for you depending on many factors. So we'll spend the next several cycles delving into these, helping you to better understand options and risks inherent in each.

Listed by class, these financing options include:

- Your own money in one form or another
- Friends, Family and Fools' (FFFs) Financing
- Accelerators
- Loan Financing
- Financial intermediaries
- Equity financing
- Crowd funding
- Asset-based financing
- Mezzanine Financing
- Grants
- Creative operations
- Initial public offerings

We'll spend the next several insights quickly delving into these, some of which you are familiar with, and some you probably have never heard of.

Let's start with funding from your left or right pocket. You may have personal assets with value above any mortgages or loans, or credit cards with credit limits that could permit you to tap into the financing they offer. You rarely need permission to do so, except sometimes from a spouse, but should carefully consider the personal liability attached to these forms of self-finance. Credit card debt is one of the most expensive possible ways to finance your business. Once you are behind in payments, charges from your card company can consume you quickly.

Personal savings certainly rise to the top of the list of methods for financing a new venture. The cost is only the lost interest or earnings of the money invested, and some amount of lost sleep from use of your nest egg in financing a relatively risky venture. But later on, outside investors, or even bank officers, will ask "How much have you invested in this?" And you'll have to face the fact that lenders or investors don't want to be the only ones at financial risk in your venture.

Friends, family members and many unsophisticated investor associates will often invest in you with enthusiasm and few requirements in return. Too many times, optimistic entrepreneurs place too high a value upon their young enterprise, or take money from those who are not legally qualified to invest in your business. We call these companies *dirty investment opportunities* when we professional investors run into these. Cleaning up a dirty company often requires lots of work, even to the extent of offering to refund early investors the money that they gave to the entrepreneur because they were not legally qualified as "accredited investors" to do so. And placing too high a value upon a young business just sets up a roar of disappointment and anger from these early investors when a subsequent, more sophisticated investor reduces the value per share to a more proper amount.

But there are many more ways to finance a young business. So let's continue to explore these.

Can you borrow your way to success?
With help from JJ Richa

There are so many ways to finance a small business. Most of them rely upon some form of debt, often personally guaranteed by the founder(s). So we investigate the most simple of these methods of debt financing first, since most are simple to execute and non-dilutive – that is help you to retain your ownership intact.

Here is a list of common loan types:
- Line of credit – short term working capital
- Term loan –real estate, equipment or other long term capital requirements
- Guarantee based programs:
  - Small Business Administration (SBA)
  - CalCap – California Capital Access Program
  - State loan guarantee
- Economic development programs such as CEDLI

The Small Business Administration (SBA) is a valuable funding resource for many businesses. However, the SBA itself does not actually make loans. Instead, the SBA guarantees bank loans, allowing commercial lenders to make loans that they may not otherwise. The SBA, through its programs, reimburses lenders for a guaranteed portion of the loan (usually up to 85%), making it less risky for them.

In order to be able to obtain a loan, SBA or conventional, you must meet the basic financial institution risk rating, which is known as the "5 Cs of Lending":

1. *Character* – responsibilities and treatment of employees and customers
2. *Cash flow* – debt handling, repayment record, debt liquidity and ratios
3. *Collateral* – hard assets, real estate, capital equipment, accounts receivable
4. – skin in the game, business resources, own risk
5. *Conditions* – economic conditions, market sensitivity ,expense management

Equity financing: great for rapid growth startups
By Dave Berkus

We've spoken of financing a young company through friends and family, known as "inside angels." There are three classes of equity investors for early stage businesses that we have not yet considered. Often grouped into formal organizations, these investors are sophisticated, helpful, and connected.

First, angel investment groups come in all sizes from a few organized angels to large groups of three hundred or more. Each has a process in place to accept applications or recommendations for investment into new companies, and to review these and make decisions based upon their exploration, previous experience in the field, knowledge of the company or industry, or about individual entrepreneurs. Angel groups invest from $250,000 to $1,000,000 or more in qualified investments.

The U.S. Angel Capital Association (ACA) lists over four hundred member groups, located throughout the country. The European Business Angel Network (EBAN), and similar organizations in other countries including Canada, all have web sites with directories of angel groups that are local to you. And even though angel groups syndicate their best deals within their respective associated networks, it is always best to apply to the angel groups nearest your physical location. If you are starting a virtual company with your employees working from home locations, as many startups do, it should be the location of the founder. All angel groups will want to see the founders in person at sometime early in the process. Being located in a distant city greatly reduces the chance of funding success.

With angel groups, you should plan of spending months in the process, from application through funding. You will have to hone your story well, down to fifteen minutes and perhaps fifteen slides in your presentation. Your opportunity becomes real when you are invited to present to the entire group at a lunch or dinner meeting, after which time one of the members or a paid group leader begins to seek commitments from the members to invest in your company. You will be given a "term sheet" during the process, calling out the terms proposed for the investment. These terms have become much more homogenized over the years, with many organizations adopting the same general form and terms offered to new investments. Your principal focus may be on the valuation of the company before the investment is made, which determines the amount of the company you will retain after the investment.

Second, there is a rather new term for those large, individual investors who are usually former entrepreneurs made rich through sale of their previous ventures. These "super angels" act alone or in informal groups, and require that you find your way to them through personal introductions from their trusted associates. The advantage to getting the attention of a super angel is that most operate informally and make quick decisions with little due diligence. This class of investor typically writes checks from $50,000 to $250,000.

The third group, venture capitalists, rarely invests in startups, usually reserving their investments for companies that have star entrepreneurs they have worked with before, or companies brought to them by angel groups or other trusted sources. VCs often invest no less than $2 million in a single deal, finding it difficult to put less money to work and still spend time on boards and coaching entrepreneurs to a successful liquidity event. VCs need much higher exit values to justify their higher amounts of investment, and often want companies they invest in to be worth more than one hundred million dollars at exit, not a riskless task.

The one thing in common with all professional or organized investors is the focus upon the exit, or liquidity event, in which the investors can realize a sale of their interest and a profit from their investments of time and money. For early stage investors, the usual expectation is seven years from investment to expected liquidity. When you take money from any of these sources, you make a pact to build, with their help, a business that can be sold or taken public, hopefully within that time period.

These professional investors look for at least ten times their invested money back upon the liquidity event, knowing that the odds of achieving that are only one in ten, and that half of their investments will probably die before any liquidity event at all. They look for businesses that are in large markets, that can grow fast, and that can achieve revenues in excess of $40 million within five years of founding. Those are difficult goals for most entrepreneurs, making this form of financing unavailable to most, but attractive to those that fit into these criteria.

Is asset-based lending for you?
With help from JJ Richa

The next logical step is to analyze asset-based lending, in which you pledge or assign your short term assets, such as accounts receivable or inventory, to the lender. Often, the lender then tracks the pledged assets until money is received or inventory sold, expecting repayment from the proceeds of sale.

Asset-based financing is a specialized method of providing structured working capital and term loans that are secured by accounts receivable, inventory, machinery, equipment and/or real estate. This type of funding is great for startup companies, refinancing existing loans, and financing for growth, mergers and acquisitions.

One example of asset-based finance would be purchase order financing. This may be attractive to a company that has stretched its credit limits with vendors and has reached its lending capacity at the bank - or a for possibly a startup company without adequate financing. The inability to finance raw materials to fill all orders would leave a company operating under capacity. An asset-based lender finances the purchase of the raw material. The purchase orders are then assigned to the lender. After the orders are filled, payment is made directly to the lender by the customer, and the lender then deducts its cost and fees and remits the balance to the company. The disadvantage of this type of financing, however, is the high interest typically charged.

Handling the reporting for such loans often require some amount of dedicated time. Many lenders require that a transaction report be generated along with a batch of purchase orders or invoices pledged as collateral for the loan. The lender has the right to reject any individual pledged item, and then calculates a percentage of the value as the amount to loan. Ranging from 50% to 80%, you can request an "advance" up to your credit limit, beyond which no more is available, and you must rely entirely upon your own devices to finance further transactions.

Each transaction report also contains a list of money received against pledged items, so that the calculation of available credit remains fresh, and based upon remaining invoices that are not yet overdue. Government invoices are usually not accepted, and any new invoices from accounts that have outstanding invoices more than 60 days overdue are usually also exempted, as are invoices to concentrated customers who account for a significant percentage of the company's business.

Asset-based financing is not cheap. Lenders often tack on charges for management of your account, for a "float" of cash to account for the number of days to clear payments received, and for a periodic audit of the company' accounts. Adding all of these often adds an additional 3-8% to the stated interest rate of the line of credit, sometimes making it one of the more expensive methods of finance.

Finally, some asset-based lenders are "factors" who actually purchase your invoices, hold back a portion of the proceeds to protect against future bad debts, then deduct their fees before remittance and remit a net amount, with the final amount to be remitted upon collection of the money owed by the customer to the factor. Factors redirect your customer's payment to the factor's postal lock box. You never see the cash collected, since the invoice is owned by the factor, no longer by you.

There are many other forms of financing a small business. Let's explore some of them.

Crowdfunding: a roar from a young lion
By Dave Berkus and JJ Richa

Can you imagine having 300 shareholders? With recent legislation and new portals on the Web, it's entirely possible, perhaps for the first time for small businesses.

Simply stated crowd funding or crowdfunding is the raising of capital in small amounts, from a broad base of investors. Usually the investors are non-accredited, and only invest a small amount. It's similar to microfinance, but for the most part using equity instead of a low-interest loan. The object behind crowdfunding is to open up more opportunities for capital to flow into businesses to help them grow and create new jobs. Participants can raise funds without having to do a public offering, which is a costly undertaking.

Crowdfunding is not for everyone. Entrepreneurs who can raise funds in more traditional ways from knowledgeable investors should still lean toward doing just that. But there are many businesses that just won't appeal to professional or knowledgeable investors. Are you an artist with a new record, a new movie idea, a new small product to offer? Perhaps you can attract a large number of investors who just want to support your idea, or get discounts for your product. The returns are not as important to them as the joy of participating in your dream. These are the more likely candidate companies and investors.

In order to participate, certain exemptions and criteria must be met, some of which are:

- No more than $1 million is raised via crowdfunding in any 12 month period; and
- No single investor invests more than a specified amount in the offering:
  - The greater of $2,000 or 5% of the annual income or net worth of the investor, as applicable, if the investor has annual income or net worth of less than $100,000; or

- o   10% of the annual income or net worth of the investor, as applicable, if either the annual income or net worth of the investor is equal to more than $100,000, capped at a maximum of $100,000 invested.
- The offering is conducted through a registered broker or "funding portal"; and
- The issuer complies with certain other requirements. Some of the important ones are:
  - o   Public listing of the name, legal status, address, website, directors, officers, 20% stockholders, and more
  - o   Share price and methodology for determining the price
  - o   A description of the ownership and capital structure of the issuer and a host of disclosures including a disclosure of various risks to investors
  - o   Companies looking to raise $100,000 or less via crowdfunding can provide financials that are merely certified as true by the officers of the company. Companies looking to raise between $100,000 and $500,000 must provide "reviewed" financials, which means they have to pay a CPA to check them. Companies looking to raise over $500,000 must provide full-blown audited financial statements, prepared by a CPA. Moreover, every year after a successful crowdfunding offering, issuers must file with the SEC and with investors reports of the results of operations and financial statements of the issuer.
  - o   The issuer must clearly disclose any compensation it pays to any person promoting its offerings through a broker or funding portal.
  - o   Issuers are not allowed to advertise the terms of the offering, except for notices to direct investors or through the approved intermediary.   Hence, all general solicitations for crowdfunding must at all times flow through an SEC-registered intermediary.

So, what are the advantages of using crowdfunding as your first effort and then going after professional investors? It does prove your business model is attractive to at least some segments of the population, a fact which would be attractive to the later investors. What are the disadvantages? Either too many crowdfunding investors and / or any non-accredited investors in early rounds will most likely cause professional investors to pass and find companies without the complexities in structure caused by crowdfunding rounds earlier.

Accelerators: a recent and positive trend
By Dave Berkus

Often I see executive summaries from entrepreneurs who have never managed any form of business, or even managed employees in their past life, and who don't know the first thing about business formation and managing for growth. I used to tell them to find a partner with knowledge in business creation and management. Although that is still a good idea in many cases, there is a recent alternative available to some entrepreneurs on a competitive basis that seems most attractive and positive.

Accelerators are organizations that selectively accept entrepreneurs into a program of intense coaching in a physical environment sponsored by the accelerator that also provides seed funds for the startup to begin its business.

Accelerators are popping up in college towns, urban cities and near existing technology hubs. Some have become well known in the entrepreneurial community as benchmark operations for others to emulate, including   TechStars and Y-Combinator. Others have a more local flavor, catering to single audiences, such as students or graduates of a nearby university.

Another term, *incubator*, is increasingly being used to define real estate operations run by universities or private groups in which the principal added value is the reduced price or free rent and access to resources from the incubator's sponsor. Accelerators, on the other hand, put entrepreneurs through a three week to three month intensive program closely monitored by accelerator management and volunteers, teaching, coaching, aiding and building the fledgling business to make it ready for its next round of financing upon graduation.

And graduation is typically marked by an organized "demo day" in which prominent investors, VCs, angels and super angels are invited to attend and see demonstrations and hear presentations from graduating entrepreneurs. There are many stories of funding deals made on demo day amid the excitement of seeing new, polished startups with great ideas and the beginnings of an infrastructure.

Are you a candidate for an accelerator? You'll give up some small amount of equity to the accelerator, receive some amount of cash in return during the program, and learn more in a short time than you'd expect from more formal education programs.

And don't forget creative fund raising.
By Dave Berkus

Let me tell you the story of how I raised $100,000 to fill a gap needed to purchase a new home for my young family years ago. I had located a beautiful home that would be a stretch to finance, and had arranged for a first mortgage from the bank, and a second from the seller. Home values were rising so fast that I knew I had to move quickly.

So I went to visit a number of customer CEOs, told them my story, and asked them to advance some amount against their future billing from me. In return, I said, I would give them more time than originally contracted for, and certainly would treat the relationship as special from that moment on. Corny? Every one of the CEOs said "yes." And I closed escrow on a home I could not otherwise afford, and which I continue to live in, after its value shot through the roof during the subsequent years.

I sometimes counsel CEOs to consider consulting to their prospective customers or in their industry while they are simultaneously developing their product for market. Consulting fees pay the bills, reduce the stress, and give people confidence in the business.

If you are already purchasing raw materials or services such as development or programming, consider asking your supplier to be a paperless partner, showing confidence in you and your future business by granting you deferred payments. You might be surprised at the positive results, if your needs are real and you treat the relationship well by following through on your promises.

How about offering prepaid licenses to your product or a package of prepaid hours, or a discount for prepayment of purchase? All of these create special relationships with your customers, who show their faith and trust by advancing money to you before receiving products or services. Just remember that you must deliver as promised, and you are eating your meal before its time. You will have later expenses to pay when the revenues have already been received and presumably spent.

Strategic partnerships with suppliers, customers and others sometimes are an attractive way to share the risk and fund an operation. Creating a new company to do this is often a time and money drain, even if it seems easier to do this than to create a relationship within existing organizations.

These are just some of the ways to creatively raise funds without offering equity or taking on new debt. Since some entrepreneurs are completely adverse to sharing equity, and some greatly fear taking on any form of debt, creative fund-raising is certainly worth considering.

Can you finance your company with grants?
By Dave Berkus

I am chairman of a company that, as I write this, is twelve years old and has not yet taken a dollar of outside investment. The company has been funded entirely by grants from the National Institute of Health, amounting to millions of non-dilutive dollars in all. The company has created a product that can be delivered as a service to medical clinicians anywhere in the world, enhancing their ability to understand their patents' problems and needs in less time, using the expertise built into an expert system created by the best minds in many medical specialties.

The company grows in value to its customers and to prospective buyers of the business, but without any dilution of control or ownership for the founders. How refreshing!

In general, grants are made to individuals, companies, businesses, organizations or institutions that are working toward serving the greater good or a greater cause. These grants include funding to educational institutions, researchers, research centers, colleges and universities, or private companies that are researching or developing leading edge solutions in several categories including agriculture, education, energy, health, medical, space, science and technology to name a few.

Grant writing takes skill and immense amounts of time. Often, grants require that you partner with other organizations to deliver the results, or measure the effectiveness of your special project. And often, grants come with detailed accounting and reporting requirements. If you can finance your enterprise through grants rather than equity or debt, you retain control and when it is time to sell your interest in the business, a lower sales price will create a higher return on your personal investment.

There are some grants available even for one person shops, from cities, corporations and even non-profits for just your type of business, especially if you support a social cause, can employ more people, or help turn around a geographic area in need of upgrade.

Both sides must be fair in a term sheet negotiation.
By Basil Peters

After being an active angel investor for about fifteen years, I realized that many of the discussions I was involved in were virtually identical to ones I'd had many times before. A good example was during the negotiation of a term sheet. These usually involve a handful of angel investors, and a few entrepreneurs, who all want to build the very best term sheet for their exciting nascent enterprise.

Unfortunately the previous experiences, and depth of knowledge of the individuals are almost always very different. To finalize a term sheet, everyone involved must come to an agreement on some fundamental principles which will have a profound effect on the future of the company. Just a few of these terms include vesting, corporate structure, governance principles, financing strategy, valuation and exit strategy.

Each one of these terms includes aspects of fairness, ethics, law, business, entrepreneurship, psychology and investing. Very often, the initial opinions of the people around the table are radically different. In most cases, these are well-meaning, intelligent people who all sincerely want to find the best solution.

Angel investing today is similar to where venture capital investing was in the mid-1980s. Back then, there was no consensus on best practices in that industry. As an example, twenty five years ago, most VCs used common share deal structures. It was not until the later 1980s that the preferred share structure became popular.

During those times, VCs had lots of conferences where thought leaders gathered to discuss term sheets, deal structures and fund strategies. As a result, there is tight agreement today on the form of VC term sheets and definitive investment agreements. Angel investing is rapidly evolving to the same state of development, as a result of networking, industry associations, and deal sharing between angel groups.

Early stage money: The problem with PPMs
By Bill Payne

The sale of equity in private companies is regulated by the Securities Act of 1933, which requires that the company either register with the SEC or meet one of several exemptions (Regulation D). A *Private Placement Memorandum (PPM)* is a special business plan defined to meet an SEC exemption. In most cases, those entrepreneurs choosing to raise capital using PPMs retain specialists (many of whom are lawyers) to write their PPMs – a rather expensive undertaking. *I don't fund new companies that have prepared PPMs for investment.* I am an angel investor, that is, an accredited investor who is assumed by the SEC and others to be sufficiently wealthy to afford to lose the investment and supposedly experienced enough to make good choices on fundable companies. Angels, as group of accredited investors funding startup companies, are assumed to meet a Regulation D exemption for purchasing equity in private companies.

Like most angel investors, I have preferences for the terms and conditions of investment and intend to negotiate with entrepreneurs on those terms, such as valuation, company structure, the makeup of the board of directors, liquidation preferences and others. I have yet to read a PPM written for a startup company that meets the parameters we angels generally establish for funding new ventures.

If I don't like the terms offered in the PPM, why don't I insist that the terms be changed to accommodate my partialities as an angel investor? Sounds simple, huh? Unfortunately, upon completion of the PPM, the first thing that entrepreneurs tend to do is sell shares to friends, family, friends of friends and other acquaintances. Then, only after convincing these "unsophisticated" investors to sign up and write their checks, the entrepreneur may approach an angel or group of angels.

The entrepreneur may have already raised half or more of the cash required in this round and is eager to top off the round. The PPM does not meet the investing terms and conditions of the angels. The valuation is too high, or the PPM is written to sell common stock when it really should have been a preferred stock deal, or other critical terms are not present in the PPM. Since many unsophisticated investors have already funded part of the round, it becomes too complicated to renegotiate the terms of the deal.

It is only fair that all capital sources in a given round should invest under the same terms and conditions. There should not be one version of terms for the early set of investors (the PPM terms) and a second version of terms for later investors in the same round. In the long term, different term sheets for investors in the same round leads to unhappy investors. We angels could insist that the entrepreneur go back and renegotiate the terms of the PPM with all the earlier investors, but the earlier investors may or may not agree to the changes. From a long history of angel investing, we have learned it is just easier to pass on PPM deals and move on to the next opportunity. We see many startup investment deals every year – too many for most of us to fund.

Regarding PPMs, my recommendations to entrepreneurs are:

- Don't prepare PPMs to fund startup rounds of investment. It is expensive and may preclude sophisticated investors from funding your deal.
- Pursue smart money, that is, sophisticated investors who will negotiate a fair deal with you and help you grow your company.
- Limit your offering: Only sell shares to accredited investors. In the long run, this usually works best for startup entrepreneurs.

Back to basics: Craft your roadmap. Plan your trip.
By JJ Richa

Business planning is a crucial part of a successful business. Business plans are dynamic instruments used on a regular basis to help owners and executives to plan for future growth, and assess past performances. Included in a business plan are financials, competitive landscape, marketing plans, and projected sales to name a few. Without a business plan, you probably are not sure where you are going, or how you are going to get there, or how you are going to know where you've been. If you don't know these things, how are you going to course-correct if things go differently than forecast?

A business plan:

- Organizes your thoughts to better run your business
- Depicts your roadmap/blueprint, and must be revisited often
- Defines your business vision, objectives and goals
- Determines financial requirements
- Keeps you on track to achieve your goals
- Helps you to be more focused
- Forces you to be more objective
- Determines feasibility
- Serves as management tool
- Assists you in raising capital

I'm not seeking a bank loan or investment. So why make a plan?

A business plan is yours alone. Bankers, financial institutions, and investors hardly look at business plans. But it's a valuable document for you. By creating a plan you are forced to think about your business and how it is structured, the objectives and other critical matters. The plan helps an owner realize how interrelated all aspects of the business are. In addition, it helps you focus your ideas and determine how to best manage your available resources including capital, cash, and people.

After completing your plan, you should be able to answer questions:

- Is there really an opportunity here?
- Can we pull it off?
- Can we make money? Is there potential for profits?
- Where are we?
- How did we get here?
- Where are we going and how will we get there?

Forecasting your finances as part of the plan will help you understand if, and how, you can improve revenue. It's hard to make changes if you don't know where you are, and where you've been.

It helps other answer the following question:

- Will they have a chance to succeed?
- Can they pull it off?
- Will the cash flow?
- Did they make any headway?
- What have they done so far?
- Will they be able to execute and reach their objectives?

As your business grows, a business plan serves as a guide to help you track, monitor and evaluate your progress. Having your short-term and long-term goals written down and in front of you can help keep you on track to reach them. Business plans provide you with the ability to identify risks to your business and what alternatives exist to minimize them. By analyzing your business objectively in the plan, you can address problems before they escalate. Studies found that people who write plans are more likely to put their goals in action and increases your likelihood of success.

Business Plans are not static. As your business changes, your original plan may no longer be as relevant. Review your plan periodically – as often as once per month, but no less than once per quarter – and make updates as needed.

Hugh opportunities do NOT command amazing pre-money valuations.

By Bill Payne

One entrepreneur has a company which appears to be scalable to a $30 million exit value in five to eight years, and a second entrepreneur's venture seems to be scalable to $200 million in exit value in the same time frame. Yet, at the pre-revenue stage of development, angel investors price both companies at a pre-money valuation of $1.5 million.

It doesn't seem right, huh?

But, it is… and here is why. It is possible to grow a company to a valuation of $30 million on one or two angel rounds of investment. But, the working capital and management team necessary to grow a company quickly to sufficient revenues to justify a $200 million valuation will require raising lots more capital. So, the angels who provided the most valuable and risky financing for the gazelle that can grow to a $200 million valuation quickly are going to get diluted by subsequent investors, probably by three to five-fold. They may own 30% after the first round of funding but will probably own less than 10% at exit. So, angels simply must value both ventures at about the same price.

Scalability is a critical factor for angel investment. Because of the risk inherent in funding pre-revenue companies, angels are unlikely to invest in any venture that cannot demonstrate the potential to scale to a $20-30 million in valuation in a reasonable time period (5-8 years).

So, angels won't fund a deal that doesn't scale sufficiently to justify investment, and they tend to value all pre-revenue stage companies at about the same valuation, which is currently about $1.5 million in most parts of the US. Although there may be some variation among business sectors, this is essentially true for software companies, medical device companies, life science ventures, electronics companies and alternate energy deals, regardless of the long term potential.

Back to basics: "What and how" of business plans.
By Bill Payne

Business plans come in several flavors, and you will probably have to create each of them to successfully raise money. Let's spend a few minutes to describe possible forms for your business plan, and more importantly, explain how to avoid common mistakes in using your plans.

Elevator pitch: A two-minute verbal description of your business. Illustrate the problem you are solving and how your solution will delight customers. Imagine you enter an elevator on the twentieth floor and find yourself standing next to an investor. How can you explain your business while the investor is a captive audience?

Video Pitch: A video of your elevator pitch that can be used electronically to introduce your business to investors. Take advantage of the media and enhance your pitch by showing investors a prototype or graphic.

Executive Summary: A one to three page description of your business, summarizing your entire business plan but emphasizing the problems customers are encountering and your solution to these problems. Entrepreneurs usually provide condensed descriptions of the competitive environment, the management team, brief pro-forma financials and the amount of capital required to start and grow the business.

Here are some more tips from Australian entrepreneur, *Jordan Green.*

PowerPoint Presentation: Follow Guy Kawasaki's 10/20/30 rule as described in *The Art of the Start*: Describe your business in 10 slides; deliver the presentation in 20 minutes using few words and large typestyle (using a greater than 30 point font).

Business Plan: A full blown description of your business. Regardless of what you read elsewhere from investors, writing a full plan is a key to understanding all aspects of the business and to creating alignment among the management team, employees, vendors, customers, partners and investors. Some investors continue to demand a full plan and often use these as an outline for their due diligence before investing.

Imagine a fishing analogy: The elevator and video pitches are lures – used to attract investors. After pitching, give those investors a copy of your executive summary. Interested investors will then set up a verbal presentation. Use your PowerPoint presentation to "set the hook." Expect lots of questions from your investor audience. Investors who wish to pursue investment will ask for a copy of your business plan and enter a stage called "due diligence," spending lots of time with you validating the investment opportunity. "Reel the investors in" and close the deal.

Don't spend too much of your time with investors talking about products and technology. Talk about solving customer problems. Why would users select your solution? Be ready to discuss all aspects of your business. Investors fund companies, not products.

Do not hand investors your business plan when you first meet them. They will politely accept it and then likely throw it away before reading. Wait until you have attracted investors and then they ask for a copy of your business plan.

Practice your elevator pitch and your PowerPoint presentation until you can deliver each smoothly. Cover all the materials quickly, leaving extra time for questions from your investor audience. It is usually the interactions during the Q&A period that will cement interest among investors.

Understand the size of your opportunity. Do not estimate revenues as a percentage of the market. Do a bottom's up analysis. Explain which customers will buy how much of your product.

Don't overemphasize the importance of "first to market." Investors know that among successful giants, like Facebook, Google and Internet Explorer, none were first to market.

Be sure to include your contact information in your executive summary and business plan. It is very frustrating for investors to meet an interesting entrepreneur, take a copy of their executive summary home to read, generate more interest by reading it and then discovering you have provided no contact information to facilitate follow-up meetings.

If further along, consider mezzanine financing.
By JJ Richa

Mezzanine is a hybrid of debt and equity financing that is typically used to finance the expansion of more mature, existing companies. Mezzanine financing is basically debt capital that gives the lender the rights to convert to an ownership or equity interest in the company if the loan is not paid back in time and in full. It is generally subordinated to debt provided by senior lenders such as banks and venture capital companies.

Since mezzanine financing is usually provided to the borrower very quickly with little due diligence on the part of the lender and little or no collateral on the part of the borrower, this type of financing is aggressively priced with the lender seeking a return in the 20-30% range.

Mezzanine financing is advantageous because it is most often subordinated to other debt, and treated much like equity on a company's balance sheet and may make it easier to obtain standard bank financing. To attract mezzanine financing, a company usually must demonstrate a track record in the industry with an established reputation and product, a history of profitability and a viable expansion plan for the business.

The rule of Thirds

By Dave Berkus

It is rare when one person starts a company, supplies all the funding, and shares no management tasks or equity with others, and still grows the company to any significant size, worthy of a multi-million dollar opportunity to cash out at exit.

We should think of the creation and growth of a high valued company as the sum of three parts, with three distinct classes of participants helping to make real value out of a raw start-up.

First, there is the *entrepreneur*, the visionary, and force behind the venture from start to finish. The reward for the entrepreneur, after years of effort, time and sacrifice, is measured by what portion of the total pie s/he retains at exit, how much the person continues to participate through that time, and how many other resources are brought in to get to that point. Most importantly, the reward is measured by how much added value the total process creates over time. It is the old story of "100% of nothing is worth far less than 10% of a large number."

Few entrepreneurs can do it alone, with subordinate hired help and no expert management to share the burdens, skill sets and efforts involved in growing the enterprise. So *co-management* is the second group to share in the bounty upon a liquidity event. Often, if not co-founders, this group is rewarded through issuance of stock options from a pool of available options that usually totals 15-20% of the total company's equity divided among all employees. Those who receive options but leave the company before a liquidity event may either purchase those shares represented by the options upon exit from the company, or lose the right to those shares, often 60 days after their exit.

The third group is made of the total number and types of *investors, other than the founder(s)*. From friends and family early on, to angels that are not related to the founder(s), to venture capitalists for larger opportunities, these investors have risked their money in the venture for only one reason – to eventually profit from a liquidity event.

It is normal for the first round of organized angels to expect to purchase between twenty and thirty-five percent of the company with their investment. Second rounds, if needed, often drive the founder(s) into a minority position, unless the company has grown significantly by that time and can command a higher pre-money valuation, giving less stock for the same amount of investment. Investments in small companies involve a much greater degree of risk than investment in public companies, which provide immediate liquidity if needed and a ready measure of value at any time. That risk deserves reward if there is a profitable sale or even an initial public offering, rare as that event is.

So remember that there are three slices to the pie to consider when creating your company and again when considering a sale or liquidity event. All three deserve recognition for the risk, time and effort in driving the company to its ultimate value.

Think of it as the *rule of the thirds.*

Find your champion.
By Dave Berkus

If you seek funds from an organized investment group such as an angel fund, venture capital entity, or even an investment club, the first thing you want to do is to find one person to buy into your vision, become excited by your enthusiasm and be willing to become the internal champion for your fund-raising effort.

In some groups, if you cannot find such a person, you cannot even find the way to apply for funding, as some groups make it imperative that any introductions come from the inside, from a member or partner. In others, if you cannot find such a champion after initial presentations to a subset of the entire group, you will not be permitted to move from initial application to the next stages of due diligence and final funding.

And in all cases, simply sending in an executive summary of the business plan via email or filling in an application for funding on a website lowers the chance of success to near nil. If you cannot find someone on the inside, network with accountants, attorneys and bankers to find a name of an influential member or partner.

You may have the most impressive plan in the world, but these organizations see tens of these each week, and often cannot be expected to understand the vision and potential of any at first glance at a document.   I receive three hundred unsolicited executive summaries a year, and my investment group, Tech Coast Angeles, sees over one thousand. Together we fund, maybe, twenty-five of these. Although much more than half are disqualified because of geographical location, industry, or amount of money needed, that still is a small percentage of funding to applications.

Banks and lenders often are the same way. Although anyone can walk into a bank and apply for a loan, those who are recommended by a trusted source are treated much more personally and have a greater chance of success.

Spend time finding your champion. Create time to network with members of these groups at their public events. Seek out names from your trusted sources.

Turn the tables: What's an angel look like?
By Dave Berkus

Angel investors, particularly those in organized angel groups, are typically former entrepreneurs who have had successful liquidity events in their pasts, or executives of companies who've retired with the funds from their stock options. Occasionally, an angel is a member of a wealthy family, having little experience managing a business. But most often these angels are skilled at growing companies, calling on their past experience to evaluate and then help entrepreneurs in their early stages of growth.

Several times in our angel group, one of the largest in the United States, we have queried our group as to their motives in being active, risking their money, taking their time to research, perform due diligence and then coach entrepreneurs of young companies. The result of these surveys over time is universally the same. Although most every angel member joins a group to find great investments that will make money for the investor-member, all have other, sometimes more personally important goals. These include giving back to the community in the form of time and investment, or learning about new industries, new advances, and a generation of new ideas. Members want to socialize with those who have similar backgrounds and interests. And members want to participate in the creation of the excitement they universally once felt in the growth and ultimate liquidity event they experienced with their previous company.

Angels come from technology, real estate, medical specialties, and many other industries, bringing a wealth of experience to the table to help evaluate and then coach entrepreneurs.

So how an angel responds to your pitch depends upon his or her background. You should try to find a way to get information about your audience before or even when standing in front of them. What industry specialties do they like, or where did their experience come from? Do you know any people in common? Are they interested in your industry either to be educated or to share their skills and experiences?

Connecting with these people often requires a bit of effort. Networking events are great starting points. Although many of these angels will appear standoffish at the start, if you can find some information from one or more of them before making your pitch, you will be in a far better place to succeed when pitching your idea to an individual or a group.

Don't over-estimate the knowledge of your audience.

By Dave Berkus

When making a presentation to a new audience, the smart thing to do, if there is an opportunity, is to ask your audience by show of hands, if they have some knowledge of your industry or space. If you are making a one-to-one presentation, don't start without a conversation about the other person's knowledge of your space. With that conversation, you create an immediate connection with your audience even before beginning to present, and you know better how much explanation you will need to accompany your most elementary statements. And you will not insult the industry experts by appearing to talk down to them.

When I give a keynote address, I often start by asking my audience, by raise of hands, to tell me how many are angel or VC investors, and how many are entrepreneurs, how many are service providers such as attorneys. Immediately, I can tell how to orient the explanations behind my pre-cast slides, based upon the response. It always works, and the audience should appreciate that the speaker takes the time to orient the talk to the audience, not the other way around.

If your audience is composed of PhD's in organic chemistry, would you want to explain the most elementary teachings in the field? On the other hand, it is most often true that only one or a few of your audience members is knowledgeable in your area of expertise. Address them directly with "I hope you will put up with me as I spend a few moments explaining some of our elementary knowledge to the others." That makes these experts a part of your presentation, able to nod their heads when you do explain these things to the others, instead of looking a bit disdainful that you don't recognize that there are experts in the room.

Don't get hung up on valuation.

By Dave Berkus

I can't tell you how many times I've walked away from deals where the entrepreneur insists on a start-up premoney valuation that is so high, no angel could expect to make a return upon the investment, even with a reasonable sales price for the company down the road.

There is always another attractive deal at the ready, and most have reasonable expectations of valuation. Why fight about valuation, or disappoint the founder at the outset? The real focus should be on smart planning, finding ways to launch and build the business with smart but frugal use of money.

Let me tell you two stories that are linked. The first is of a 2004 startup that I cofounded and led the investment group for several early rounds, then VC rounds. The company has grown to forty employees and a healthy eight figure gross revenue run rate, but has absorbed over $36 million of angel and VC money to do so, and without yet reaching breakeven.

The second story involves the same founder. This one is using outsourced development, support, outsourced customer relations and more. The total capital raise will have been under $600,000 if all goes as planned, and the founder retains majority control of his baby through this and even one optional future round.

For the first, company, the founder's remaining portion is under 4% after all the subsequent rounds, and not yet at breakeven. The second company, with the same founder, finds him with majority control even if the original raise is not enough. For the founder to see any return at all in the first company, the ultimate selling price must be above $40 million. In the second company, better planned, the founder would be made pleasantly wealthy at a selling price of $10 million. The chances of the latter occurring are much greater than the former. This founder was not hung up on valuation for the second company, just upon efficient use of capital.

Don't be defensive, but defend.

By Dave Berkus

When meeting with investors, during the period devoted to feedback after your presentation, you will hear comments and recommendations that don't resonate with you. Some will be from a misunderstanding of your explanation. Some listeners will challenge your assumptions. Some will seem to ask just plain show-off questions, in which the questioner wants you and others in the room to know that s/he knows more than you do.

You are in a vulnerable position in that room, the salesperson looking for money before individuals who have nothing to lose but risky profits far in the future. You cannot appear to be standoffish, or above responding to some of these inappropriate questions.

Defend your position when appropriate. But listen carefully. Although you may be completely right, the questioner's comment may indicate that you are not getting your points across. That's just as valuable for feedback as hearing a good, new idea.

Sometimes, you will have an opportunity to present to several levels of an investor organization, from first prescreening, to a screening session with many present, to the final meeting of the members or partners. Plan to incorporate the appropriate responses to earlier questions in the presentation to avoid those being repeated. Show that you are both humble and adaptable.

Investment groups including venture capital fund managers will tell you that the very process of defending your plan will help you better think through the rough spots, better launch the business with fewer holes in reasoning, and better connect with resources that can be used to accelerate your growth to breakeven and beyond. The process is always time-consuming and grueling. But approached correctly, the time is well spent and the results almost always positive, even if money doesn't come from the present effort.

Create a ten percent profit model.
By Dave Berkus

Most entrepreneurs, when starting to model their business operations using a spreadsheet, start with expected revenue by month. Then they calculate cost of sales, and then project their expenses, to find the bottom line profit or loss each projected month.

There is a rarely-used twist that makes lots of sense. Add a new row at the bottom of the spreadsheet. Project your revenues and costs as in the original exercise. Then consider that an operating entity should be able to generate a ten percent operating profit based upon revenues, and add a row to your spreadsheet immediately below "operating profit" that calculates 10% profit from sales each month. Compare that with the operating profit as calculated, which surely will be lower, probably negative, for months or even years. The difference is something new – a target for reduction of expenses or addition to revenue for each month in which the calculated number is lower than 10% of revenues.

We are not taught to think this way, but rather to find the month in which we break even in our plan, then calculate the accumulated losses to that point, add all the cash needed for investment in fixed assets, and end up with the amount needed to finance the business to breakeven through equity or debt financing. This new tool gives you that number *plus* the amount needed to make the business a viable entity with a chance of long term survival. The longer the time it takes to break even, the higher the number of dollars needed. Sometimes, the difference is a reminder to consider a reduction of expenses, if revenues cannot be raised from projected levels.

And sometimes, it is just a reminder that we are all in business to make money, not to break even. Just like assuring that your own at-market salary is included in a forecast even if not drawn in cash during the earliest periods, the 10% target reminds us all that the target must be higher than merely breaking even, even if that means reassessing all expenses until the target is met or exceeded.

Chapter Three. MARKETING and POSITIONING

Things are changing at a rate never imagined even five years ago.

This is a new world for product development, marketing and demand creation. With all the noise created by small businesses able to look and act like their big business competitors, the message you give to your potential customers is now much different and potentially powerful than ever before.

Attention spans have reduced as the amount of information bombarding us all has increased. We all must assume some of the expertise of a marketer today, since most everything we say or do becomes public knowledge quickly. The Internet has an infinite retention span. Bad publicity, poor positioning, and bad marketing efforts will remain out there for a very long time to be found by competitors hungry for an advantage, or customers looking for validation.

So in this chapter, we attack some of the issues in which you must become an expert, or at least be knowledgeable. We will not attempt to teach you "how to" do something, but rather to guide you with expert advice and insights about what to do, and why.

The three legged stool of marketing excellence
By Dave Berkus

Marketing is a science devised to help drive customers to your door. There are lots of ways to define how to market well, including the four P's of marketing (1): *product, price, promotion and place.* This is considered to be the producer-oriented model. These are still the driving focus behind most marketing courses, and deserve to be so.

Then there is the four C's, the consumer-oriented marketing model (2). The four Cs: *Consumer, cost, communication and convenience.* This makes sense too, and surely deserves time.

Oh boy. Then there's the compass or cardinal definitions model for marketers: *N=needs, W=wants, S=security, and E=education.* We can go on forever. But I have my own model that is even simpler.

I'll call it my IDC model, just to fit into the scheme of the conversation.

I= increase revenues. Find a way to position the company and the product to be wanted so much that it moves into the needs column for the consumer. Use all the techniques you learn in marketing classes to drive demand. Higher demand results in higher prices - if there is limited supply. Or, with or without limits on supply, higher demand results in greater revenues, satisfying the "I" in the formula.

D=Decrease costs. With greater demand comes the option to increase production and gain efficiencies of scale, driving costs down in the process. Even without higher demand, reducing costs should always be a focus for management to provide breathing room for increased profits.

And finally: *C=Customers, and more customers.* Marketing should provide a pool of ready to listen customers, no matter what the price or complexity of the product. More importantly for management, finding a way to focus on extreme customer service will be the most inexpensive, effective marketing tool of all. Existing customers have low acquisition costs, addressing the "D" in the equation. Extremely happy existing customers are the greatest marketers you will ever have.

Increase revenues, decrease costs, and better serve customers. IDC: that could be a motto or even a manifesto for any good management team.   And it's a good place to start a focus upon positioning.

(1) First proposed by Jerome McCarthy in 1960
(2) Robert Lauterborn, 1993

The LALA School of marketing
By Dave Berkus

While we are at it, let's focus not upon the process of marketing and positioning, but on you. How should you become the best marketer you can be, even if you are a first time entrepreneur or a seasoned CEO?

There's an answer for that. The title of this insight helps us find a formula: LALA.

Listen! The first rule of marketing and positioning is to listen to the marketplace. Interview potential customers, hold focus groups, meet with existing customers. Hire consultants. Attend trade show education sessions. Ask you field representatives to debrief you about what they are hearing. But listen!

Adapt! Create, change, throw out, tweak or put more resources behind those efforts or campaigns that are working. Listening does no good without action. And the first thing in marketing is to adapt your product or service to the needs of the marketplace.

Learn! Measure the results of your changed program in as many ways as possible. Create metrics for customer acquisition, retention, conversion, reach, or anything that helps you to better understand the effects of your changes to the program.

Adapt (again)! It's not unfair to reinforce the cycle by again adapting to the market after learning from your changes. Start the cycle all over again, and never stop.

LALA: Listen, adapt, learn, adapt.

Do you really want to be the first to market?

By Dave Berkus

Over the years, as I managed my several computer companies as CEO or executive chairman, I made the decision to go to market with a brand new product that had never before been exposed to my customer's marketplace. In each case, after overwhelming publicity, certainly noticed by a great number of potential decision makers, and after record-breaking sessions at industry trade shows to introduce these to the potential buyers, the products failed in the marketplace.

I recall the introduction of artificial intelligence into the hotel reservation process, a "one-up" on the airline method of yield managing the price of airplane seats. With the cover story in the industry trade journal, record-breaking overflow education sessions at the international trade show, and even glowing reports from the first hotel user's management, the product failed to attract more than two customers and had to be withdrawn from the market, even though it was an unqualified success for the first users. As a side note, we returned to market with the application as a software-only product without artificial intelligence and without some features, reduced the price from $150,000 to $8,000, and had a subsequent hit on our hands.

In another instance, we introduced the first kiosks for hotel lobby check-in. They were large, a bit clumsy looking, and gathered cobwebs in the lobbies of some great hotels.

These and other efforts to be first over the years have led me to ask my current crop of CEOs as I serve on various boards, "Do you have the resources to evangelize the market, educate your potential customers, AND sell your product?" The answer is invariably 'no,' because the cost of evangelizing a new product is completely unknown. A marketing professional or the marketing department certainly can work to obtain good press, appealing to curious journalists and early adapters. Early meetings with potential customers will yield enthusiasm for a "free test" of the new product. But if it is a radical departure from the comfort zone, the cost of promoting and marketing the new product will be beyond the capability of most small or medium sized companies.

Even Apple rarely attempts this, with all its resources. Apple is well known for building upon the work of early adapters. After failing with its early Newton tablet, Apple waited for fifteen years before reinventing and repositioning the tablet as a much friendlier consumer device. The same occurred with the iPod. Apple was not first or second. They just added the infrastructure needed to seamlessly purchase and download content to their offering, and produced a friendly way to use a product that previously required early adapters to manually download songs to their devices.

I will readily admit that the half million I spent on the artificial intelligence system that failed generated the greatest positive press we ever had. As a corporate promotion, it was a hit. As a product marketing effort, it was a failure.

If you are going to be first in a market, plan on a very long time from introduction to acceptance. Triple the time you estimate for the effort, and add four times the cost you estimated for marketing.

Does anyone know how much Toshiba lost with its HD DVD format marketing effort? First to market over blue ray with what some say was a better product, Toshiba dropped over a billion dollars into that one and lost it all. There are numerous examples like that one.

You might be an exception. Chances are that you'd do much better by inventing a better mouse trap, and marketing it for its advantages over a product that the consumer already understands. But there is always a winner at a table with the odds stacked against the player. It just doesn't happen often enough to expect success.

The "drop dead" question for a customer survey
By Dave Berkus

Sean Ellis, the marketing guru behind DropBox and other successes, advises clients that "The most important question on a survey is, 'How would you feel if you could no longer use this product?'" He goes on to quantify the response. If more than forty percent of the respondents say they would be "very disappointed," the product should go viral and be a great success. Conversely, if less than ten percent say this, those companies or products would have a hard time getting traction in the marketplace.

What a great test. It reminds us that our customers, especially early adapters, must want to continue to use our products to the extent that they "would be very disappointed" if unable to do so in the future.

What other questions could we wrap around this critical one to form a great survey that is both short enough and powerful enough to be relevant to our marketing effort, let along our R&D and production efforts?

Using Sean again as a source, we might ask: "How did you discover our company?" and provide several checkbox answers, including 'friend or colleague.' Again, it is a sign of a viral marketing effort to get more than forty percent checking that box. Then "Have you recommended our company to anyone?" Use just 'yes' and 'no' as possible answers, and look for more than fifty percent 'yes' responses.

And there is always the great open door question: "Would it be OK if we followed up by email to request a clarification to one or more of your responses?" If more than fifty percent say "yes" you have a real hit on your hands. It means you can use this respondent as a resource for case studies and marketing quotes in the future.

Keep your survey very short to insure a large number of responses. But do include at least one specific question about your product to be sure the respondent is an actual customer.

Use video whenever possible.
By Dave Berkus

Ninety percent of all traffic on the Internet is in video form. Yes, most of that is from NetFlix and YouTube and others delivering entertainment content. But an increasing amount is now coming from web sites and YouTube videos created by companies looking for an edge in their marketing efforts. The average time spent on a static website, one without videos linked to the home page, is under a minute. That time more than triples when videos are positioned to be delivered with just a home page click.

Videos are no longer expensive to produce, even though a poor amateur effort may be much worse than none at all. One way to create great company videos inexpensively is to contact your local college or university and ask if there are interns signed up for such work with local companies. Another is to combine clips you've accumulated into a professionally edited video without creating any new shots.

Each video, especially those on the front page of a site, must be compelling, to the point, and short. If you are selling a product, a one to two minute demo that is well edited will work wonders for viewer retention. If you are promoting the corporation as opposed to the product, short clips of the company's previous projects with comments from enthusiastic customers would be appropriate.

Finally, content does not last forever. Videos should be replaced or rotated at least annually to be effective over time. No matter how many videos you have to offer on your site and on your YouTube channel, videos will increase your marketing awareness.

Only those in the fight can win.
By Dave Berkus

Entrepreneurism is all about risk. Sometimes, you can reduce your personal risk by taking in other people's money, starting with a contract from a customer, purchasing a going business, or spinning off an existing revenue-generating portion of an existing business.

Even then, the risks of having enough cash to fund daily operations or growth can be daunting. The same is true about marketing. If you don't directly engage the potential customer at the right time, place and mood, you are at a disadvantage from the start. There are too many competitors for a customer's time and money to make an error in your approach and offer.

But the truth is in the headline. If you don't chose to enter the fight, it is impossible to win it. And entering the fight without the proper resources usually assures defeat. Resources such as money, experience, statistics about your target, experienced marketing and sales talent, and especially a compelling need and attractive product are all important to the ultimate success of an enterprise.

So ask yourself: Are you ready to enter the fight? Do you have the resources necessary to at least give you a chance to win? If not, what do you need to do so, and how can you get those resources?

I am often surprised at the inexperienced executive's estimates of time to breakeven for a product or a company, about the time and cost to market, about the expense in overhead needed to stay in the game. Most of all, I am surprised at that typical person's inexperience in the marketing arena, and understanding of the importance of marketing to the success of the product.

You may have all the other ingredients. But without an excellent marketing plan and a way to execute upon that plan, the best product and the most cash reserves won't bring in the customers. Since great marketing means addressing the wants and needs of the customer, about distancing the product form any competitor, about getting the message out to the most people possible, you've got to commit resources and energy to the fight in order to have a chance to win it.

Use "switching costs" to your marketing advantage.
By Dave Berkus

Know the cost to move from your existing platform, and estimate the switching costs for moving from a competitor's product or service to yours. Offer incentives to existing customers to stay, and for competitor's customers to switch. Protect your base with incentives to stay that are intangible - such as membership in an insider's club, access to special deals not available to others, and attention from the executives at the top.

The momentum from an old decision that took lots of effort to implement is worth something to a marketing professional. To keep an existing customer, even if by offering discounts, is much less expensive than the cost of attracting a new one. To reduce switching cost from a competitor is to lower the barriers to a quick decision that might have been otherwise much harder to make.

Increase the barriers to your customer's switching, not just with excellent service, but with some form of personal touch. Recognizing a longstanding customer with an appropriate gesture from the top is best of all.

Recently, I received a hand-written letter from two co-CEOs of a company I had helped out with a few hours of time. They accompanied the letter with a customized gift of their product that contained the logo and name of the college where they knew I was a trustee.

First, I have not received a hand-written letter other than a greeting card from any business associate in what feels like decades. I was in such shock, I did not respond in kind. What should I do? Pull out a piece of stationery that had been sitting unused for over a decade and write in longhand? You aren't supposed to respond using a less personal vehicle than the original one. So email was out. A phone call might have done it, but not with the elegance of the original correspondence. Now, every time I turn from my desk to the credenza behind, I see that letter and gift. I am not willing to just file the letter or put the gift on the shelf. That's the power of a great outreach from the top.

And that's a lesson for all of us in marketing. Find the right way to reach existing customers that stands out from the usual. Find an offer that makes switching easy for others. Pay attention to opportunities to differentiate yourself from the rest.

Someday I will file the letter and put away the customized gift. In the meantime, those two guys got many more miles from a relatively simple gesture than I would have thought possible.

Embrace the right to pivot!
By Dave Berkus

Plans don't often work as devised. We are not always smart about the market or the product. Great teams are not bound by their original product or marketing plan. Greatness finds one definition in management's ability to "pivot," or change the plan in reaction to its early response from the marketplace.

Investors celebrate teams that quickly find the flaws in the original plan and reallocate resources in another direction before more wasted effort. Even the term, pivot, seems to call up images of a light-footed dancer able to move so very quickly in any direction.

My favorite example of a world class pivot comes from the CEO and board of one of my most successful investments. Green Dot Corporation was formed by an entrepreneur in the year 2000 to create a product to permit those without credit cards to purchase items on the Internet. Think of it: to shop on the web, you must have a card, not a nine digit routing and bank account number. The young, inexperienced entrepreneur had two assets that attracted me – rights to use the MasterCard name on this new product, and a laser focus to make this work in any form possible.

Over the years, that vision changed dramatically several times as the world's first debit cards were invented by the firm, positioning the card to be used by the un-bankable, those unable to obtain credit cards or in some cases even checking accounts. The firm grew to dominate its new field, create an infrastructure to allow any of its 70,000 retail stores to simple activate or load the card with money from any cash register. It replaced Western Union as the preferred way to send money across great distances. And it built a billion dollar market and then some - where it might have been restricted to a small percentage of that.

And we who held early stock celebrated together the ringing of the NYSE opening bell the day that often pivoting company went public.

Lighting the match – going viral
By Dave Berkus

It doesn't happen by accident. Not every new game site is a Club Penguin. Not every social network is a Facebook. Not every texting application is a Twitter.

What are the elements needed to focus upon in making the attempt to take a product viral? Intrigued by the thought, I recently made a list. It was as much in reaction to my getting blank stares from entrepreneurs when I asked that question as it was for me to better understand the problem itself. Here is my list.

First: *Planning*. Retail or end user web sites do not even receive limited notice without being discovered through a real marketing program, aimed at finding the flywheel effect (the moment of going viral that makes all the difference between failure and success.) In today's world of social marketing, it takes someone knowledgeable if not expert in understanding how to use available resources in promotion and marketing.

Second: *channels*. I am chairman of a company that distributes its product through over one hundred fifty retail Internet travel channels, all websites where someone else spent the money attracting their users and attempting to go viral. We could not have begun to reach a fraction of that audience with any amount of money if we did not reach through these channels. Sometimes, it is just the right idea to brand your product inside that of a known presence.

Third: *cost*. Even a great marketing plan to gain an audience fails if there is not enough money to prime the pump. And of course sometimes that requires a large amount, far beyond the capability of small companies looking for its initial audience.

Fourth: *measurement*. If you can't measure the results of your attempts to gain a viral response, how can you know when to focus upon reinforcing or changing the effort? Well-tuned metrics are an absolute must. And the tools for most are available, sometimes free, for the educated marketer.

Fifth: *reaction*. If everything goes right in finding the right plan, channel, cost and measure of success, and if you do nothing to reinforce the success or change the focus, the rest of the effort can easily die a slow death.

And sixth: *the pivot*. A reaction is not often enough. Many times, it takes an intelligent repositioning of the entire offering to try again from the start with revised ideas based upon learned experience.

It's a cycle that must be learned and followed in order to successfully maximize an opportunity in any industry and for any company. So, where in that cycle are you today?

Chapter Four. MANAGING YOUR WORKFORCE

No-one can do it alone. Even small businesses need help from experts on the outside to safely grow or protect the business. In this chapter, we explore issues relating to managing, recruiting, developing a board of directors, dealing with your associates and more.

We are often told that our workforce is our most important asset. If this is true, to be a great manager of people is right up there in importance with creating a great product or service. The culture of the company you help to create will outlast you, if you do it right and reinforce it with training at all levels. Workplace satisfaction, efficiency, retention and recruiting all depend upon your mastery of the art of workforce management.

Here are numerous insights as to how to build that legacy and create that lasting culture, starting at the first moment of contact with a new employee.

"Over-welcome" your new employees.
By Dave Berkus

A CEO friend of mine who manages her one hundred person remote workforce as a virtual company told me her story of how she welcomes new employees as she grows her firm. *Strike that.* She over-welcomes her new employees.

Days before the official start date, she makes sure that the new employee's business cards arrive in the mail, that the employee's phone and Internet services are up and running, and that an email account is already established. But many of us do that, maybe not so timely.

Then she topped her explanation with: "A few days before the start, a package arrives from us at the employee's home with a welcome letter, a copy of the CEOs book, and a giant fortune cookie, with the fortune cookie message streamer clearly visible."

"You will be successful at our company!" the fortune states.

What a great touch - especially for someone expected to be self-motivated enough to work long hours from home, to get to know fellow employees through Skype and texting, and to be productive immediately when hitting the ground.

It started me thinking. How many days or weeks or even months do we expect a new employee to take in becoming acclimated to our company and its culture, to the marketplace, and to our ways of doing business? For example, most of us expect a salesperson to be truly productive only after about six months of building a territory or client base. But isn't there a better way to approach this expensive process of acclimation?

For a salesperson, how about paying an override commission to another sales person for a short period to help find and close new business? Or how about helping the employee gain confidence by handing the first several accounts to the new person ready to close? How about assigning a big brother or sister to each new employee to show them the culture and process? How about teaching a class in corporate culture yourself to one or more new employees? Some of us have done one or more of these things. But what could we have done better to launch a new employee successfully?

Maybe we should start with a surprise fortune cookie with a personal welcome message.

Two very powerful words: Great job!
By Dave Berkus

The best managers we all know are the ones who take the time to praise good work in public, before an employee's peers. Most of us have a monthly award for the top person in a group of employees. And if we are big enough to formalize the process in a regular meeting, we make it a regular part of that meeting.

If you haven't already discovered this fact, such a process quickly becomes routine and predicable. Small companies have trouble finding new people to honor after a while. Some employees even disingenuously consider the process an exercise in pandering, discounting the effectiveness of the award, and disenchanting those very managers who thought they were reaching out to do a good thing.

For all of us, we should remember that the best possible way to honor great work is to do so immediately. A "Great job!" coming at the right moment from the boss is valued as an honest recognition of good work, especially if done in front of an employee's peers.

At times, it is an entire team that deserves the recognition, again immediately after doing a great job. I found a formula that worked for me where most of the employees were in several buildings on the same campus. First arranging for my assistant to obtain the appropriate amount of hundred dollar bills from the bank, and then to follow me around checking off names, I had my own personal holiday celebrating each individual in the team with a handshake, words of thanks, and a C-note. With lots of laughter and thanks, the celebration and words "Great Job" made for a completely memorable event. And those pop-up thank you visits from the boss certainly contributed to the culture of the company. Word does travel.

Remember to reward those not present at the moment, and remember that the amount should be grossed up to take care of taxes and be entered onto the payrolls of the employees so rewarded.

I'm sure you have your own way to making "Good job!" work for you and your team.

Some great coaches are younger than you are.
By Dave Berkus

Especially for social media-based businesses, we all need to recalibrate our thinking about who is the teacher and who is the student. There is nothing wrong with a manager slowing a conversation to ask for more background when speaking to an often-younger and more involved associate. You know what I mean... The conversation goes something like this: "We found it on x site and using y app with z as our data object."

First, managers could not be paid enough or have enough time to stay entirely current with all of the details each employee or associate deals with daily. Yet, many times that other person tries to explain an important finding or breakthrough, or make a significant comparison, using names of destination sites or apps or tools we have never used or heard of.

Yes, age often has something to do with it. And occasionally, a manager has to work to join the club by trying new things, learning new tasks and using new language to relate to those already in the know.

I recall vividly one such experience. I helped to found an Internet game company, playing the role of founding investor, chairman and even temporary CFO. The company was destined to grow into a large, very valuable enterprise that we sold for many, many times our investment. But that first day with the new employees was a test for me. Many years older than any of them, their initiation was to insist that I spend no less than forty-five minutes playing for the first time first person shooter games against Internet-based foes. I had to acknowledge the difficulty of achieving high degrees of skill, and the size and terminology of the extended gamer community. But most of all, I had to gain acceptance as "one of us" in an environment where my CEO coaching and my money did not count.

That was a lesson for me. Taking the time to be taught by those able to master a skill or have extra knowledge is an important step to show respect for everyone at all levels in an organization. And that respect flows in both directions, worth so much more than the time it takes to learn a skill or terminology or meaning.

Stealing time

By Dave Berkus

It's a big issue within any company. With easy access to Internet shopping, games, social networks and more, employees are able to find many ways to focus on personal issues while at work, detracting from productivity and demonstrating a dis-respect for the time paid for by their employer. In fact, if we were to be direct, we might label it "stealing time," and consider it a crime of sorts.

Based upon the actual "loaded" cost of an employee per hour, that is certainly not an insignificant cost for the employer. Certainly it amounts to many times the cost of stealing something tangible, such as a ream of paper from the supplies cabinet. Yet, many of us treat the latter much more severely than the former.

Let's consider counter arguments. Attracting great employees often requires us to offer special incentives, including flexible hours, unsupervised time off, and access to perks such as free food and soft drinks. Often, employees just expect some degree of freedom when they work, to be able to quickly shop or communicate with friends in the middle of their day. In times past, older generations were perhaps more discrete when making personal phone calls (how ancient this sounds). But they often did so anyway, and often spending more time and more company money in phone bills than today's typical employee distraction.

How about the counter to the counter argument? There is no way to sugar-coat the fact that paid time is for work, not for outside play. The cost may seem small until someone calculates the combined cost over a year of time and screams "thief!"

As in all two-sided arguments, there usually is a middle ground. The boss who requires complete adherence to the work-every-minute ethic called for in the employee handbook generates ill will when enforcing the rule. But the manager, who openly ignores the behavior, encourages more of it from employees who will fall in to follow the example they see openly acknowledged.

My solution is to acknowledge the fact of life, equate it to personal time once used for personal calls, and define a 'limits of acceptability' publicly. "We recognize how difficult and intense your work is. We think it prudent for you to take breaks as often as every hour if you need them. We expect your breaks to be self-policed and no longer than ten minutes, to be used for all personal issues including personal use of your workstation. Remember not to stray out of bounds of corporate decency and confidentiality, and be safe in protecting corporate security."

Extending Your Runway
By Dave Berkus

Several years ago, I wrote a book entitled, *Extending the Runway*, using parallels to piloting a plane to equate to the process of creating and building a small company, making maximum use of resources to get to and beyond breakeven. It is worth revisiting the most important point of that book, which was written to prompt discussion between entrepreneurs, professional managers and their boards of directors about issues that could unite them or strain the relationships between them.

There are five types of resources a great board can add to a company. These are: *time, money, relationships, context and process*.

Time: The longer it takes to produce and release a product, the more fixed overhead is consumed, and the runway of remaining cash diminishes. Expert help and good planning can reduce the time to market, saving cash in the process.

Money: A board of directors is primarily responsible for oversight in the use of and the raising of money for the company. There is a fine line between loading the company with too much debt, and diluting the shareholders too early with additional equity investments. But all agree that a good board will express its stewardship well by preventing the company from running out of money.

Relationships: One reason for having an effective board is to give the CEO a resource for tapping into great relationships that are owned by the various board members, so that the CEO can reach out and find help in areas most needed. If a board member has few appropriate relationships in his or her field of expertise or from past experience, then perhaps the board member is not appropriate for the company at this time. And if the board member refuses to volunteer or allow such relationships when needed by the CEO, that board member should be held to task by the other members of the board.

Context: Every good board has recruited at least one industry expert, often as the fifth or mutually-approved outside member. With expertise in the company's industry, that person can and should provide expert advice about the timing of the company's product entrance and applicability in the industry it addresses. A great product at the wrong time or a poor product unable to address the needs of the industry will fail in the marketplace. That board member should be actively involved in questioning the positioning, marketing and even the design of the product to avoid just such a disaster.

Process: Here, most experienced board members can help to streamline the process of product development, manufacture, channel management and marketing. Knowing how to scale from test to release or how to complete a process more quickly saves money and time, making this knowledge as valuable as raising more money for the company, but without the cost in dilution or debt.

Use your board to help you to navigate through control over these five resources. If you don't have a viable, relevant board, build one no matter what your size and stage of development. One thing is usually sure: an entrepreneur cannot successfully do it all alone.

It's about time.

By Dave Berkus

While we are revisiting the issues raised by my earlier book, *Extending the Runway*, we should examine the challenges to a CEO in making use of enterprise time, one of its most valuable and often misused assets. Enterprise time, as opposed to personal time management, is defined as the sum total of resources available to a company expressed in terms of time – time to develop, to debug, to produce, to deploy, to respond to issues, and to make changes in plans that are not working.

By reducing the amount of time to perform any of these actions, the company saves fixed overhead and increases profit or reduces cash burn. So this issue becomes one to be dealt with by every manager at every level of the organization. Building efficiency into every corporate activity should be a corporate mandate, one to be discussed interdepartmentally, to be refereed by the CEO.

There is the flip side to making efficient use of time. I've labeled this *time bankruptcy* to make the point as dramatically as possible that this is a critical, company-threatening sinkhole that must be avoided at all costs.

Time bankruptcy is the ultimate result of the deliberate over-commitment of a company's most valuable resource(s) by the CEO or a department leader. There are many ways to fall into this trap. But the first thing to do is to identify what those critical resources are in your company. Most often it is the time of the chief architect of the product or service you provide, or of the best developers of that product. Sometimes it is the time of the CEO, which when overcommitted, prevents others from gaining access to solve critical problems or continue the flow of production.

One way to fall into the time bankruptcy trap is to release a product too early, and pay the price by forcing the architect and most skilled developers to drop off of their important tasks to put out fires in the field and fix problems one at a time.

Another is to fail to complete a contracted service for one customer and to do so multiple times, until many customers begin screaming for attention, drawing away all available talent from new, income earning tasks.

You will surely be able to identify an example of time bankruptcy that you have experienced in your past or present. It is your job to drive the company out of the time bankruptcy zone and to watch for signs of it occurring in the future, stopping the process before it becomes critical. That means watching quality control efforts more carefully, developing metrics to track incomplete processes and track remaining time committed to completion, watching the number of customers exposed to a new product or service before general release, and more.

It also means being careful that you, as a senior manager, do not become overloaded to the extent that you are unavailable or inefficient in helping those who need your attention to complete their tasks. Use the term, time bankruptcy, in a planning session, and see what response you get from your managers and employees. You'll be surprised at their understanding of the issue as it relates to their being able to complete their tasks successfully and of their contributions to solutions that will benefit everyone and increase process efficiencies.

Finally, enterprise time equates to available runway, or remaining cash and resources that you can call upon to gain market share and increase corporate value. Spending enterprise time inefficiently burns those resources unnecessarily. If you have enough reserves in cash and in time, you can dig out of the hole. But if you are managing a marginal business, the effective use of time as a resource extends your ability to make changes, reposition, react and build.

So if you wonder why we focus on this subject to the extent of seeming redundant, well then, *it's about time.*

Back to basics: Boards of directors protect and help to grow the enterprise.

By Dave Berkus

No matter what your size, if you intend to grow your business into more than just a lifestyle workplace, you should create a board of directors. If you take money from knowledgeable investors, you will be required to create a board as a part of the investment process.

Boards perform two important types of task. They protect the company by overseeing the expenditure of company money for expansion, acquisitions, purchases of large assets, hiring of senior management and more. A board is usually composed of a mixture of the senior executives or the CEO, at least one representative of the investors, and at least one industry expert from outside the company. The usual size of a board is five, but legally the number in most states is equal to the number of shareholders up to a maximum of three board members required by law. With three or more shareholders, you must have a three person board of directors in most states. The average board for a company taking outside investment money is five. Beyond seven members, a board is often too cumbersome to be at the most effective value to the CEO.

Each board member is legally tasked with two duties: the duty of care, and the duty of loyalty: care for the living entity that is the corporation itself, and loyalty not to the board member's constituency, but to the corporation itself. Sometimes, these duties conflict with the best interests of the board member personally or his or her co-investors. This could happen when a board votes to take in new money at terms that would be unfavorable to the class of investor represented by the board member. It could happen if some early investors and board members want to sell the company at a price below the objective of the later board member, where the relative returns are excellent for the early investors and marginal for the later ones.

There is no legally-mandated requirement that members of the board help a corporation to grow. But it is certainly the goal of the investors, the CEO and even the board members individually, when assuming the position of board member. Often, a board meeting is entirely devoted to issues of growth, with members chiming in to help the CEO with marketing issues or customer acquisition.

It is important to make time for the required duties at board meetings. Approving the budget and watching over it during the year, and approving any actions that would dilute ownership including stock option grants, are two examples. Much less understood are issues that address the management of risk, such as review of corporate insurance policies, adherence to OSHA safety regulations, and oversight of the terms of real estate and large equipment leases that could affect a company's ability to maneuver in times of crisis or extreme growth.

Many entrepreneurs would rather not have to answer to a board, and resist creating an entity that could have the power to check management actions, and even to fire the CEO in extreme cases. Yet, the establishment of a proactive board is the first step toward professionalizing the company and its management. Properly handled by the CEO with adequate time allocation for individual and group board member updates, the proper use of the board will help control risk and provide resources to management that will pay back in better overall management of the company and more efficient use of its resources. More importantly, no entrepreneur or CEO can do it all alone, especially in a rapid growth scenario. Too many things can go wrong, many of which are things that one or more board members have already dealt with in their business lives.

Take the establishment and nurture of a board of directors seriously. It is much more than a legal requirement to be resolved. It is the creation of a vital part of the organization, one that could be of great help in both protection and growth of the enterprise. Great boards create value for shareholders while protecting them at the same time.

Be sure the Board and CEO are in alignment.
By William De Temple

Boards of directors have the power to hire and fire the CEO, even if the CEO is the founder of the company. That's not only a daunting prospect, but it is one that can result in more than just misunderstandings between board members and the founder of a company.

Sometimes, because this very issue could destroy or damage an enterprise, it is most important to understand and prevent. Here's a true story that will scare any founder taking money from third parties. But don't be too afraid to read this. We'll have some insights into prevention in just a bit.

The company CEO had worked hard for three years and developed strong relationships with nine major retailers nationwide for a series of new products which had a quick return on investment of between nine and twelve months. There was over $2 million of angel capital invested in the company, with the entrepreneur-CEO initially investing several hundred thousand of his own money.

The company's new products were patented, and they were completing beta tests at user sites from which the company had received its first order for just over $65 million, based on an expected three year roll out.

An angel investor who had a seat on the board concluded that the entrepreneur-CEO didn't have the experience necessary to take the company through what appeared would be the rapid growth curve about to come. At the next board meeting, without any prior notice or discussion, he proposed replacing the entrepreneur with a mature, seasoned CEO - completely blindsiding the entrepreneur and the rest of the board. After hearing the board member make his case, the board agreed with him that the entrepreneur-CEO did not appear to have the experience necessary - and voted to replace him.

Removed and shaken, the founder-CEO initiated suit, and both parties ultimately agreed to binding arbitration. The advocate board member even argued during arbitration that the entrepreneur's share of the company was unreasonably high, and requested a redistribution of ownership of the company.

Somehow ignoring terms of the investment agreements, the arbitrator ruled in the favor of the investors, and affirmed the board's decision. The entrepreneur lost control of the company and his job in the company he founded. A new mature, seasoned president was brought in to manage the company as planned by the board. That would be the end of the story if not for a subsequent event.

The board failed to take into account the strength of the relationships built over the years between the entrepreneur and the company's major customers. The advocate board member was elected chairman of the board, and took on the responsibility of negotiating the terms of an employment agreement with the new president. However, the two were never able to agree on the final terms of that employment agreement, in spite of the new CEO already starting work.

At the local airport, on their way to a major meeting with a customer preparing to enter into a significant contract, the new CEO demanded that the chairman sign the employment agreement he thought he had negotiated, or he was not getting on the flight. The chairman refused to sign "with a gun to his head," and the CEO never got on that flight. The contract with the major new customer was never executed. Word spread through the retail community. The original retailer cancelled its $65 million order. The company soon closed its doors.

What went wrong here? First, there was no orderly discussion of the issues between the advocate board member, the full board, and the entrepreneur. Properly presented, the entrepreneur might have concurred with the position for the sake of increasing value of his own founder stock. Properly handled, the board might have granted the entrepreneur the continued position of chief visionary, head of business development, or any title and responsibility that would have best served the company and its needs. With that, he might have been happy to step aside and add a seasoned CEO to the company, for the benefit of his equity value and that of all others. Instead, the confrontation destroyed all good will between the founder and the board, making a sharing of knowledge and transfer of customer relationships impossible.

Second, no one on the board role-played the effect of the decision upon the customer community, or planned how to handle the transition in its many forms, including ongoing contract negotiations. There are times when a transfer of power is an emergency, or is strategically vital to complete with a precise and very sharp knife. This was not one of those, and the company suffered the ultimate loss of value as a result of that decision not to seek an orderly transition.

There is a message here for boards of directors and entrepreneur -founders. It is always best to communicate early when there are concerns, and find a way to achieve mutual goals in the best way possible, even at the expense of some duplication of effort and payment of additional cash during a transition. There are almost always ways to reduce the emotional impact upon the one most affected by such an action. And it is always best for all to avoid the costs and stress of litigation.

Don't make assertions that will later prove untrue.
By Dave Berkus

Sometimes it is easy for someone at the top of an organization to make a statement that, in the enthusiasm of the moment or to make a point, crosses the line between fact and fiction. Sometimes it seems to you to be just an unimportant little stretch of the facts. An estimate of the number of customers, of the amount of traffic to your website, of the numbers of products sold or hours spent in development - there are thousands of areas where a number sounds better when it is larger.

Often, the number you state cannot easily be challenged, sometimes justifying the use of a larger number as a way to impress at potential customer, or make a point at an industry meeting.

In this age of readily available information, the risk involved in making a statement that can later be proved untrue is too great. It goes to your credibility itself when discovered or challenged. And often, when someone discovers or uncovers the truth, you'll never hear of it, even as that person lowers his or her trust in your future statements by some level as a result.

Yet, we have all done this in one form or another, some harmlessly, some with intent to deceive. An often-expressed example seems to come from the salesperson who quotes a larger number of users or customers than the facts support. Yes, we've seen gray areas. In one example in an industry I know well, there are direct customers and then central systems that in turn support direct customers. The company in mind provides systems to serve both, but its salespeople count as customers all of the indirect customers served by the one system sold to oversee them. The result is an inflated number of total customers, which when compared to the competition counting only direct customers, makes the company look much larger and with greater market share.

Is there any harm in this activity? Yes, in two ways, this hurts credibility and confidence. Competitors have every incentive to research the truth of your statements and every incentive to broadcast findings of inaccuracies. And the creator of the knowingly inaccurate statement will always be a bit wary about being challenged, sapping just a bit of energy away from other communications with the same constituents, and knowing that a previous statement is vulnerable to attack.

It is best just to not make those statements in the first place. They probably don't do the job expected in enhancing the person's or company's reputation as intended anyway.

Attack critical issues first.
By Dave Berkus

There are two reasons to consider reordering your priorities to attack your most critical issues first, before the easiest ones to knock off the list.

First, you are fresher at the start of a day, and your best efforts should come when you are best prepared to address these issues. Remember how easy it is to put off those final decisions at the end of a tiring and long day?

But the real reason to do this is to allow most everything else to fall into place, once the critical issues are worked out. It's true in every business, all the time.

Take for example, solving key technology problems that prevent a product from shipment, or from scaling to large production. If sudden demand for a product takes management by surprise, having solved these key issues will remove the key barrier to ramping production and taking advantage of the opportunity.

In a young company, the key issue is most often finding the way to start the revenue flowing from services and sales. With enough revenues, the young company can more easily raise equity funds, borrow money, hire top talent, and gain valuable publicity.

Next, a critical key issue is finding the way to break-even for a young business – the proxy for stability. Working on that issue alone can drain a CEO, given its many incarnations - in marketing, sales, finding efficiencies, cutting efforts that are of lesser value, and more.

Hire key talent to develop the product, to create a manufacturing line, establish distribution channels, to organize the sales effort, and you will find that many other less important issues resolve themselves or fall into place, much less important than before the critical issues had been resolved.

Back to basics: Three qualities of a great leader
By Dave Berkus

There are lots of ways to measure a great leader. Here are three that should resonate with you as leader and with those who follow you. These qualities are applicable whether you are leading your company or a board, and certainly are aspiration targets for you if you are measuring yourself against the best.

The first quality in a great leader is to have *laser focus.* Every organization has limited resources, especially money and time. So a leader who is able to focus upon the core needs of the organization, eliminating all the surrounding noise, is one who uses the limited resources available to best effect. McDonald's does this by focusing upon good food, delivered quickly. There are a million examples of great companies and their leaders focusing like a laser on core components of the business and succeeding where others failed because of the inefficient use of limited resources.

Second is *consistency.* It is more than difficult to follow a leader who changes course seemingly without reason, or sets standards that change by day or by whim, or rewards one person or department differently than others. Inconsistency breeds fear, disillusionment, and discontent among those suffering, following this flaw in leadership.

Third, a great leader establishes goals that lead all *to maintaining forward progress.* Stagnant companies lose their best employees, those wanting a challenge and upward mobility in a growth environment. Forward progress can be felt by all and celebrated as the company reaches new milestones toward its goals.

Measure yourself against these three qualities. Have the courage to ask a board member or even a direct report to comment on your three measures. Where do you need a bit of work? Not one of these requires formal education. So there is no excuse for failure to be your best in all three qualities.

The five tactical skills of a great executive
By Dave Berkus

While we are on the subject of great leadership, let's list the five principal tactical skills of a great leader. These are not the strategic visionary skills, like leading companies through risky product launches, or steering the course through economic storms where leaders become oversized personalities for their superhuman efforts. These are the skills of daily operation, the ones that make or break a company - from the top.

Think of those leaders from your past or present whom you respect most. Compare their leadership style with these five skills.

Skill number one: *delegate*. Nothing is more of a turn off to a subordinate than having the boss do the work for that person. Worse yet, failures to delegate make the leader the principal bottleneck in the flow of work through an organization. A great leader learns to delegate, first.

Second: *measure the results* of delegation. If there is no attempt to measure, no-one will know if the work is up to standards for timeliness, quality, or the vision of the leader. There are many types of metrics, some very easy to manage. But failure to find and use them regularly is a failure at the top.

Third: *support*. A leader's duty is to make sure that anything s/he delegates and measures is given a chance of success by providing the tools required to perform the job. Those include funding, people, training and facilities.

Fourth: *reward*. A great leader is a great cheerleader, knowing when and how to reward effective achievement through all levels of the organization. People naturally work for rewards, from simple recognition to financial incentives.

Fifth: *celebrate*. There is no greater feeling than to achieve a goal and to celebrate that with some form of out-of-the-ordinary event. It can be a simple handshake and comment in front of others who count, or an all-company celebration after achievement of a major goal. A leader who fails to follow through and celebrate misses a major opportunity to enhance the culture of the organization and motivate the troops to further achievements.

Delegate, measure, support, reward and *celebrate.*

If it can be counted, the CFO owns it.
By Dave Berkus

There is a simple way to define the responsibilities of the chief financial officer. And it extends beyond the usual interpretation of the CFO position in many companies. *If it can be counted, the CFO owns the responsibility for controlling it.* The CFO should question and control the number of *anything*, including the number of chairs to be ordered. That may seem extreme to many a CEO, but it serves a purpose. It is the ultimate control over rampant spending or uncoordinated purchasing.

Looking at it that way, there is a check and balance for all departments and individuals ordering materials of any size that affect the cash position and profitability of the company. Further, the CFO should speak up in executive meetings and when invited into board meetings, making sure that any major issues are vetted by the group.

I was an early angel board member of a company that subsequently raised over $30 million in venture money following the angel rounds, which themselves amounted to $6 million. I remained on the board through the life of the corporation, a witness to some surprises along the way that were, at the least, instructional. First, the VC's ordered that the company ramp its burn rate (monthly losses in cash) to over $800,000, which I could not fathom. But it was their money and they must know what they were doing, I thought, as I watched what I thought to be all-or-nothing spending. The CFO dutifully followed the VC commands to spend, and managed the spending process well – even if it exceeded reasonable standards of control over the ever-increasing inventory, headcount, and fixed expenses as the infrastructure grew.

But the CFO let the spending rate continue to increase out of balance with the board-approved budget which projected revenues to ramp, reducing the monthly cash burn. In one four hour board meeting with all in attendance, the board spent almost an hour with the CFO analyzing the financial performance of the company. We never saw, and he never mentioned the balance sheet and cash position. It was eight months after the latest $11 million round and no-one thought it worth focusing on cash, since the position should have been over $5 million in cash and starting to grow - if on plan.

A week after the board meeting, the CFO emailed the board that the company was only weeks from having no cash in the bank. Can you guess the board's reaction? The CFO was immediately fired. I performed a forensic audit on behalf of the board to determine if there had been any fraud or theft; but there had been none. Spending had continued out of control, much of it for inventory and assets - neither of which appear on the income statement. So those expenditures were not reviewed by the board which had not been given a balance sheet to examine.

The moral is simple. A CFO is responsible for all phases of cash deployment and preservation. Failure to manage to plan, and failure to inform the board of dangerous excursions, caused this company to fail as the VC's decided ultimately not to continue to pour money into the investment.

Maybe the CFO could not have saved this company; but he surely could have slowed the flow of cash, informing the board, and giving the board and CEO the opportunity to pivot the plan, to reduce inventory, to reduce spending, or to consider looking for a strategic partner or buyer.

Especially in companies where the CEO or founder is not a financial expert, the CFO is expected to be knowledgeable, willing to confront as well as inform, and to find early warning metrics that help in the process of effective cash management. That person is not a bookkeeper, counting the past, but an expert at forecasting and control.

Be an Adaptive Business Leader.
By Dave Berkus

The title of this insight happens to be the name of a CEO roundtable organization I belong to, and have been a member since 1989 *(Adaptive Business Leader Organization – or ABL)*. The organization, like Vistage, manages roundtables of CEOs meeting monthly in small groups, where they discuss their mutual challenges and help solve each other's complex problems, acting as an informal board of advisors. Unlike other groups, ABL members all belong to either healthcare or technology industry-focused roundtables. There they not only discuss their business issues, but significant business-changing trends facing their industry. Since I am chairman of the Technology side of the Organization, I attend more than one ABL group each month, and estimate that I've now attended more than four hundred half-day roundtables over the years.

Why would I spend so much time networking with other CEOs, discussing mutual problems and solutions? The answer is that I am the recipient of many insights from fellow CEOs that sometimes strike like lightning bolts when least expected. It was an Internet CEO roundtable in early 2000 where it became obvious before the public was aware, that the bubble was just beginning to burst for such tech businesses. And it happened again in early 2008, as CEOs reported the first evidence of order slowdowns and issues with customer payments – right before the 'great recession.'

But most importantly, it is the constant hearing of stories by these CEOs of how they were able to adapt to changes in their environment and alter the course of their leadership, adapting to external influences that had changed in their industry or the economy.

At each session we hear one of the dozen or so members present in depth, requesting feedback from each member of the group in response to a list of concerns that is explained during the presentation as background for the help hoped for from the group. I contribute my two cents of advice, as do the others in the group. As an active, professional angel investor, often I can help in areas not familiar to the others, when fundraising issues are on the list.

There's the story of the member-CEO who saved her company during the great recession by dismantling its fixed overhead, sending everyone home to work virtually, and building a new culture to successfully support over one hundred workers from home. Her recruiting business survived and flourished even as others closed their doors during the recession - and have remained shuttered.

Ten years ago, a young entrepreneur joined one of the roundtables, and we followed his progress with his issues, many of them directly related to fundraising, as he grew his company from a raw start-up to an initial public offering on the NASDAQ exchange, followed by continued growth in revenues and stock price. During the early years, he often asked for advice about funding, comparing various sources and offers, threading the needle between the wishes of the investors and his judgment as to how to grow the company.

Somewhere along the way, as he grew his company to a size larger than any others around the table had ever managed, we became the students, listening to a set of concerns that were often stunningly beyond any we had experienced. With a small stake in his company, and monthly contact through these roundtables, I happily find myself the former teacher, now the student.

The theme of these roundtables is "adapt" – to be ready for and embrace change quickly and efficiently in the light of opportunities and changes that might be missed by other CEOs without trained antenna-like skills.

You, too, can be an adaptive business leader, if you spend time with your ear and nose to the ground, listening and looking for signs of opportunity and change, then acting quickly to accommodate or take advantage of limited windows in time. It is a skill that can be taught. More importantly it is one requiring that you spend some amount of your time looking for signs of change. Many of us are locked in the daily grind of our business, and default to managing events and reacting to incoming stimuli, such as emails and internal requests for assistance.

An adaptive leader seeks out change and embraces the opportunity to take advantage of trends early in their cycle, or to reconstruct a business in response to early signs of trouble or weakness.

Start by paying more attention to indicators of change within and outside your organization. Gather information to support your observations. Then act when appropriate to secure the advantage or protect the enterprise.

Seek out a roundtable organization if you can, to find a group of fellow executives ready to share and solve your problems of the month, or share theirs with you to better inform you of those you might otherwise miss in your management life. It is certainly worth the time and effort to hone your skills at becoming an adaptive business leader.

You may burn your first professional manager.
By Dave Berkus

It seems to be a rule, not an exception. The first professional senior manager that an entrepreneur hires to share the growing workload does not last more than a year. Why?

Entrepreneurs start businesses with a strong vision of *what and how*, involved in every process from buying supplies to hiring and directly supervising early employees. The culture of the company is built day by day by those actions, often centering on the founder's vision and management style with little room for deviation.

At some point, as the company grows, either the founder's span of control is stretched to the limit, or investors enter the picture, often with a clear idea of how they would like to scale the company to grow quickly. This happens predictably, either voluntarily in the case of the founder deciding that s/he needs help at or near the top, or involuntarily when investors insist upon the addition of professional leadership.

If this new executive hire is the first for a founder or founding partners, and if the person is expected to relieve some portion of the that executive workload, there is a predictable and great risk that the first person hired to do so will last only a short time at the company.

I've seen this happen so many times, it is almost a rule for me. I warn the entrepreneur to be careful in the interview process, to expose the candidate to people at all levels of the company for buy-in, to be absolutely sure that there is a culture fit. But most important of all, I warn the founder that s/he must be ready and able to let go, to delegate clearly, and to establish metrics for measuring the performance of the newly hired executive – but not to interfere with that person's day to day management unless absolutely necessary. I urge the founder to coach, but not to expect the new executive to be a duplicate in style or perceived ability.

It is an unhappy but common occurrence: the recently hired and trained professional manager is let go, and a new search started. Luckily, in my experience, the second person hired for the job often is much more successful – usually not because the person is better at the job, but because the founder is more willing to delegate, expecting less a duplication of self.

If this is so common, is it not possible to be aware of the probability, and condition yourself to be more tolerant of someone else's different style of leadership? It might be a learning opportunity for the founder, often coming from one more experienced in the position and in growing company leadership.

Hire slowly. Fire fast.
By Dave Berkus

New hires can shore up the weak areas of a business in ways existing employees cannot, if hiring is done to fill true needs. Some employees lose their drive, or remain behind as the company grows, failing to gain the experience or knowledge needed to manage expanded processes or numbers of subordinates. Sometimes, there is just too much work for one person, and a second is needed to continue growth. And of course sometimes, a person leaves the company, creating a need to fill a hole.

There is a rule few follow. Slow down and take more care in the hiring process. Vet the candidates well, even though you think that you do not have time enough to do so. Hiring is one of your most important duties, a way to increase the quality and productivity of your company's staff. Every hiring opportunity is a window to improve the company. Hire slowly, with the weight of that opportunity clearly in mind.

On the other hand, we are all guilty of hanging on to marginal employees for too long. It is humane; it is easier to do nothing. It is less of a drag on your time to let marginal employees continue to plug along in their job. We have all done this. And yet, we have all looked back after a painful separation of a marginal employee, and thought that we should have made the move to replace the person much earlier. We agree that the person would have benefited with a better fit, and the company would have surely performed better having hired the replacement earlier.

It is human nature to hire as quickly as possible, to reduce the time taken from a busy day for interviews and reference checking. And it is human nature to hang on to marginal employees. Both are opposite the best practices of good management.

Try to force yourself to slow down in the hiring process, and speed decisions you know will someday have to be made about marginal employees.

The five "Whys"
By Dave Berkus

This is a trick headline. There can be three "whys" or twenty, depending upon the issue and the responses. To make the point, the word "why" has to be one of the more powerful words in a manager's vocabulary. Asking the question forces the other person to think beyond the usual "what" what generated a response to "why."

It sure is a way to get to the bottom of an issue. "I just reduced the number of ad words we're paying for." "Why?" "They weren't paying off in enough revenue." "Why?" "Well, all we could measure is dollars of revenue against cost for clicks." "Why?" "Well, we have no way to know which other ad words might have done a better job of conversion into revenue." "Why?" "We have no-one on staff with enough knowledge of marketing to distinguish words from phrases, or with experience to know how to capture clicks into conversions." "Why?" "We've never thought this to be an important part of our marketing effort." "Why?" "We just don't know what we don't know. Will you stop asking 'why'?"

How revealing! There is no better way to get to the bottom of an issue than this. In the case above, lack of performance was caused by lack of knowledge, and inability to find resources to help. A good manager-questioner might conclude that a small expenditure with a consultant might pay off in great rewards, before abandoning the use of ad words entirely as a result of the comment from the subordinate.

Practice your listening skills with one or more attempts at the five "why's" and see if you find insights into answers to problems that might not have been obvious without your queries.

Stay in touch with your investors.
By Dave Berkus

Investors as a group have a common gripe - almost universal. Information flows from the company irregularly, in fact most often when the company is urgently in need of more money.

Investment documents usually call for quarterly reporting by the company to the investors. Less than a quarter of companies receiving early stage investment voluntarily fulfill this promise. Usually, one or more of the investors is placed on the board as a requirement of the investment documentation. The entrepreneur often expects that person to keep fellow investors informed. And sometimes the board member does perform the service. But most often, the CEO or founder has a much better idea of the flow of quarterly activity than a board member meeting monthly or less often, and for a relatively short period of time. More importantly, the investors want to hear directly from the CEO.

Many times, companies need another round of investment, and the first people approached are the same ones that invested the first time. If they have not been kept informed about the progress of the company, and if they are surprised by the fact that the company has run out of money more quickly than planned, it is a much harder sell to obtain the next round than the last.

Rob Wiltbank, Ph.D., of Willamette University, is one of several academics who have followed multiple rounds of investment in a significant group of early stage companies. The typical finding is that second round investments are not as profitable for the investor as the first round. So investors are more cautious as a result when approached for additional money if not kept in the loop between rounds. If a company is meeting milestones and growing as projected, and if the CEO is diligent in keeping the investors informed, a second round is much more likely to be raised from the early investors. But the studies include all second rounds, including those that were pulled from investors reluctantly to protect their first money in, skewing the curve away from more heavily weighting successful conclusions.

Keep your investors informed. Avoid late surprises. Plan financial needs early, and inform investors early of that plan. Explain problems encountered and solutions undertaken. You and they will benefit by this candor and communication.

You are watched more closely than you think.
By Dave Berkus

Ever had a manager above you who said one thing and did another? At least once? Or in a pattern of repeats? Well, you're not alone. Did you think less of that person for it? Would you follow that manager to the ends of the earth? Well, almost everyone has had multiple such an experiences with a senior manager. And most people think less of that person than before.

On the other hand, think of the professional you most admire. Do you know of any times that person has made promises to you and missed on delivering them? The difference comes down to trust and respect. We lose both when we catch someone, especially someone above us, acting differently than his or her self-proclaimed rules, or even violating company rules.

It is one of the most vital elements of good management – restraining oneself when rank would ordinarily grant special privilege, and instead acting as one would expect a subordinate to act.

Black and white examples include taking supplies home, using company time to perform personal duties (if not permitted), and even traveling business class at company expense on short trips. Larger and more important examples involve direct promises that are broken, such as review dates with implied raises, or promised follow-through on an issue of great urgency to person receiving the promise.

Everything you do as a manager is watched by one or many. The very culture of the enterprise is shaken when someone in power gets away with bending or breaking the rules expected to be adhered to by all. Why have rules, or a company handbook, or new employee orientation sessions if the actions don't match the words?

And once violated, it is almost impossible to retract the action. That should make us think twice before taking small liberties.

Do you tell your direct reports HOW to do a job?
By Dave Berkus

Unless your job is to teach, attempting to tell your direct reports HOW to do the job you've asked or ordered them to do will be a disincentive, will remove some of the authority you've delegated, and definitely reduce their motivation to act and lead.

Think for a moment of sometime in the past where someone directed you to do a job, then launched into a lengthy explanation of how you should do it. How did you feel at that moment? I'd bet that you were either silently or openly angered that the person assumed that you didn't know how to do a job even before asking if you did. This has been true since we were kids, and dad told us to rake the leaves, and then launched into an explanation of what tools to use and how to do the job. If that happened to you in some form over the years, I'll bet you pushed back immediately with something like "I know how to do that, Dad." You felt diminished by dad's assumption that you didn't know how to do the job.

The same is true in business, even if there is less drama and far less confrontation exhibited by the respondent. It is perfectly logical for that person to ask for help, or to a lesser extent to immediately offer it without a request. But it is a grand disincentive and personal affront to force upon a respondent a short lecture on how to do a job without being asked.

Most of us would think that it is just good management to provide another tool – teaching how to complete the task when asking for it to be done. Not true. Remember dad's doing that to you years ago.

It is a lesson in understanding human pride and dignity. Don't include "how" when you tell a person "what" and "why," unless they ask for help.

Don't manage with "what" without "why!"
By Dave Berkus

Empowering your direct reports with the reasons for your orders gives them incentive to act, motivation to accept authority, and purpose behind action. I try to teach this with the simple phrase that is the headline of this insight.

Think of the last time someone above you in your business or personal life gave you an order to do something that seemed either illogical or of low priority - to you. If you accepted the authority of the person giving you the order, you just performed the task, probably either wondering if that person was nuts or whether you just didn't understand the reason for the task.

What if that person had told you why it was important to be done, in clear terms that related to that person's priorities? Wouldn't you be more prepared to perform the task knowing the context?

I just spoke with an old friend who is in sales. He lamented the fact that his boss recently layered several more sales reports on him to complete each week, reducing his selling efficiency. How many times have we heard this complaint, especially from sales people? I suggested that he go back to his boss and explain that it would be more than just helpful to know why these new reports are needed, that even though the salesman has no need to know, it would certainly make doing the work less of a chore. And by the way, I offered, if the boss could not explain why, there might be an opening to advance the argument that the trade in time between completing the new report and reduced sales call time might be worth a revisit of the order.

How many tasks, reports, and rules hang around the necks of people throughout a more mature organization, which remain as "what" without anyone remembering "why?" It is probably as effective a tool for the manager as for the recipient of the order, to explain *why* when telling *what* to do.

Your employees will appreciate the small extra effort, better understand the reason behind the request, and perform the act with more enthusiasm. What's not to like about that?

Help your employees to grow through their position.

By Dave Berkus

When we accept the work commitment from a person we hire, we make a pact with the new employee that often stops at agreeing to pay for service rendered and to provide a safe working environment.

There should be more than that. With some people you hire, you know you are just renting their services as they pass through your organization, aimed at a higher calling. Others want to know that they are signing on to a career, not a job, and expect to move up within the ranks or on to a larger company that can accommodate their goals.

A recent statistic I saw surprised me. But as I thought of examples of people I know, it seemed more accurate than I would have imagined. The average new college graduate today will work thirteen jobs in his or her career, in an average of five different fields. Ouch! What happened to a job for life? How can employers expect complete loyalty if there is no clear upward path to the top for the best new hire?

The answer coming from the best of breed in corporate personnel management is to form a trusted bond with that openly-identified employee, helping that person to manage his or her career within and preparing to follow the company experience. If a superstar agrees to work for you for a period while learning the ropes to move to a better job elsewhere, assuming that there is candor in the communication by the employee and a level of trust in and by the employer, it is perfectly proper to offer to help that employee succeed. The pact between employee and employer is that the employee gives the best possible service to the company, in return for the company helping the employee to grow in, and perhaps beyond the position.

Especially with young entrepreneurial CEOs, this feels to them like a stick up. "Give me your money, and I will work only until I find a better job." And that attitude might be warranted if the employee just performs to the minimum required level, marking time to the next opportunity. But if the person has skills and knowledge that the company needs, there is the basis for a fair trade of talent and time for a later organized, positive move to the next level outside of the company.

With that openly positive corporate attitude, you can celebrate the growth of the employee with a party as the person graduates, instead of either feeling anger when an employee resigns with short notice, or being suspicious that the employee will leave with trade secrets in tow. Certainly other employees will see the supportive behavior, understand the company's contribution to the career of this upwardly mobile employee, and celebrate not only the graduation event but the great culture of the company itself.

Are you too emotionally involved in the decision?
By Dave Berkus

Negotiating an agreement, especially one that involves personal gain, is tough for the person personally involved. There is too much to lose to be objective, to be willing to walk when terms go upside down.

It is my experience that you should have an expert negotiator with you or even in your place, whether from your board or an employee or outside professional such as an attorney – when the issue is personal.

Think of buying a car, for example. If you are looking for your spouse or offspring, it is probable that they've picked out the perfect car and are ready to take it off the dealer's hands. Assuming that you are the elected as or self-assigned to be the negotiator, the last thing you want is to have them in the room while you haggle over price. Advantage other side.

Negotiating on behalf of business associates too personally involved in a transaction: it's a role I've played tens of times over the years. There are the several that were disengagements between partners threatening to sue each other for perceived wrongs. There's the sale of a company, where as a board member, I asked the CEO to name his asking price and then go home and wait the result.   There's the disengagement with an angry employee threating to sue the company.

All of these are personal issues to a CEO or founder or entrepreneur. And all of them draw that person emotionally into making decisions that cannot easily be objective, or into finding solutions that are mutually acceptable without the torture of constant re-explanation of opposing positions.

A smart lawyer, they say, should never represent himself. And yet, lawyers are trained in the art of negotiation. You should be careful not to miss the point of that admonition.

My oldest son learned to accompany me, but keep a deadpan look on his face as I negotiated for his ideal car, completing the purchase in minutes. The CEO described above endorsed his company selling for twice his asking price, after his absence helped the negotiation to be completed within an hour. The partnership described above dissolved without suit after a personal visit by the negotiator without the first partner present resulted in settlement within an hour. The employee just described accepted a severance check in trade for a release, without the emotion of arguing out old issues between employee and employer.

Are you too emotionally involved in a decision? Consider the advice lawyers give each other, and find a surrogate to argue your case.

Fire yourself. Rehire a new you.
By Dave Berkus

When a new CEO or manager is hired into a company, for a while lots of energy flows from the top and new ideas seem to be generated daily. It is one reason not to fear the unknown when upper level management long in place turns over, often leaving most everyone worried about the future of the company and for their own prospects.

Even the best of us fall into a routine in our jobs. It is human nature to do so, but it is not a sign of our best efforts. We recall the enthusiasm we had for the job earlier, how we couldn't wait to get to work, or initiate a new plan, or share a new idea. We can be that person again. It just takes a bit of effort to change our mindset.

We may run out of fresh ideas after a time; most of us do. But there are sources of great ideas right next to us in our own company, or available to us from fellow CEOs, or from industry consultants with a broader view of the landscape, uninhibited by our need to meet daily obligations.

One of my most respected CEOs arrived at his monthly CEO roundtable meeting years ago and announced that he had just fired himself. He had reconfigured the company, delegating many of his previous responsibilities, and rehired himself in a new position more strategic to the company, retaining the CEO title. It was an attitude adjustment, self-initiated. He credits that effort as the start of his company's real growth, resulting in a great public company, dominant in his field.

Another CEO described how he drove to work each Monday morning forcing himself to think of what he would do if he were a newly hired CEO, fresh on the job that day. He surprised himself with his many fresh ideas, just with that change of perspective.

However you do it, refresh yourself. Be that new CEO - but with all the knowledge and skills you already have as a head start.

Protect your outlier innovators.
By Dave Berkus

Here's one for executives of technology companies, or any company with next generation products in mind. As your business grows more complex and there are more employees to manage and more customers to care for, slowly you will notice that more and more time of your chief innovation officer or system architect or R&D department is spent focused upon enhancements in response to needs of the user base.

The company's most valuable technical visionary, the person tasked with staying out in front of new technologies, developing the next generation of new products, and thinking "a mile above the box" is drawn into working on projects that are incremental to the product and to the existing business. Often he or she will approach you and state that the work has become more boring, and that there is no time left for creative thinking or next generation experimentation and development.

That's one scenario. In many companies, there are people who are quiet geniuses, wanting to work on projects outside of the daily focus of the department or company. Managers sometimes view this behavior as non-strategic or wasteful, and even sometimes will isolate or reject these outside thinkers outright.

Or finally, you may want to start a project using the next generation of tools to produce an entirely new product – but your development resources are all tied up with projects to enhance existing products. Whichever of the three scenarios may apply to you, it is a red flag for your future if you condone the status quo, and allow the company to devote all of its resources to existing products and simple enhancements. Your best creative thinkers will leave you, looking for more challenges than you can offer. Your competitors may already be working on the next generation of product, as you remain stuck in the mud, even if focused upon serving the customer base with outstanding service and rapid feature rollout.

It is up to you to decide if research and development for advanced or next generation products is a strategic priority for you and your company. If so, you have a duty to protect these future-focused developers or architects, removing or reducing the pressure of reactionary development work, and isolating them in a space that prevents constant interruption by others focused upon day-to-day work.

Technology companies are prime targets for this problem. Every six to ten years, there is an entirely new platform to focus upon for the next generation of products. Just think of the computer and software fields. First there were mainframes, followed by minicomputers, then client-server systems, then peer-to-peer networks, then the Internet, mobile devices, cloud computing, and now mesh networks. Each generation required new tools, rewrites of software, creation of new user interfaces.

And in each generation, there are dominant players from the past generation that fade as new companies not inhibited by the demands of their user base leap beyond the last generation's leaders with new systems for the new age. Leaders of significant size are sometimes made irrelevant over time, or pivot into service organizations, or absorbed into growing next generation companies.

What happened to Wang, Sperry-Univac, Burroughs-Unisys, DEC, RCA, and hundreds of early generation leaders? Their CEOs did not provide enough of a safe environment and enough resources to their creative geniuses to make the leap into that next generation.

It is a cost of doing business that you cannot ignore. Not only providing resources for next generation development, but protecting the people performing those development tasks should be one of your strategic priorities.

A tale of two CEOs and the management of pain
By Dave Berkus

This is the tale of two CEOs, one of them unfortunately....me. It's a story of how people handle unusual situations when selling to the top – an executive of a prospective customer. And the stories couldn't be different.

Recently a CEO friend told me her story of a dinner with her director of business development and an executive of a major company, a candidate for a large sale. As the dinner progressed, he started, and then continued to excuse himself from the table, looking paler each time. After several of these, upon his return, she asked him is everything was OK. He responded, like most of us would, that all was OK, and that he was having a bit of trouble breathing, would probably have to leave the dinner early, and drive home.

She took one more look, and went into decision mode. "No, you aren't fine," she stated. "Give me your car keys; we're going to the hospital." He reluctantly acquiesced, and she tended to him as her director drove all three to the hospital. She had him call his wife on the way to meet them at the hospital. As they waited in the emergency room, after more episodes, his breathing finally became easier, and by the time the doctor saw them, he could find nothing of worry, ruling out stroke or heart attack. Our CEO then returned to the restaurant and met with the chef to have him list all the ingredients from the meal the executive was eating. The problem was, as you guessed, an undiscovered food allergy, with a possible ambulance ride averted and a happy ending. The executive even tells the story now that the CEO may have saved his life, because he was unwilling to own up to the fact that his breathing was so very difficult.

Now, I would not have been so fast to take charge. Maybe it's a guy thing. I would have been thinking about the sales relationship and the sale, and would probably have let the guy drive home, acknowledging his discomfort, and ending the dinner early.

This leads me to my story. Years ago, I was in the process of selling a $125,000 system to a well-known baseball hero who owned his namesake hotel in St. Louis. Flying on the red eye to make a morning appointment, his hotel bus driver dropped me off in the dark a few feet beyond the lighted portico. I stepped off the van into... a recently dug pit about two feet deep, and broke my foot in the fall. What pain! I tried to sleep in the room they gave me, and managed to make it to the 10:00 AM meeting with the very well-known sports figure and sales candidate. He saw me drag my leg into the conference room, made no comment, but asked if I would like a tour of the hotel. "Of course," I said, ignoring the pain and dragging my foot the entire way through the tour.

Well, I didn't make the sale. And I didn't sue the hotel. I was in selling mode and nothing was going to detract from my focus or reputation. I sure was not admitting to the problem or seeking recourse for the obvious flagrant error by the hotel in not marking the excavation.

Who was right? Well, I should have led the meeting with my story of woe in order to protect others. The other CEO took charge, and made a friend of both the potential customer and his spouse, who she called as they drove to the hospital.

Is it a guy thing? Is it conditioning us to put things in perspective regardless of the personal outcome, including a lost sale? I think about these two examples now, and have concluded that there are some traits of a great CEO that cannot be learned easily. Putting others above self, and sacrificing a short term goal is not easy for a type 'A' driven entrepreneur when the stakes are high. *But it is the right thing to do.*

Power is sometimes assumed when not granted.
By Dave Berkus

How many times have you heard someone say "Let's do it now and ask permission later?" It's a common practice in companies where there is a barrier between levels in the chain of command, or lack of communication between contemporaries. The statement represents a failing at some point in the delegation or communication chain by a higher level of management, and should be taken as a warning that there is a problem greater than the issue handled at the moment.

I've worked with organizations that are so large that extensive paperwork is required to obtain approvals to accept customer orders, make any purchases of any size, or any commitment of resources. In every case, people try to stretch those restrictions in as many ways as possible to get around the time taken to complete forms and lost in waiting for approvals. It's the "order prevention department" syndrome.

Incomplete delegation of responsibilities, or controls that are too tight, both lead to a rationale for subordinates to circumvent the system. The worst thing about this is that the people most likely to do this are those most entrepreneurial and creative in doing their jobs. Conversely, those most likely to fall back and seek guidance, clarification and direction are those most subservient and least creative.

Middle managers sometimes identify those who assume power as non-conformists or even troublemakers. It is rare to ever see a dialog come out of such an event that leads to better defined delegation of responsibilities, removal of roadblocks, or relaxation of overly restrictive rules. More often such actions lead to reprimands without analysis of the underlying general cause. And occasionally, the very creative, driven individuals you would otherwise celebrate are made candidates for elimination instead of catalysts for change.

Reward success and failure. Punish only inaction.

By Dave Berkus

Reward failure? That may be a difficult concept for an executive. And there are limits of course. We wouldn't reward a failure to follow laws, or protect lives, or deliberate endangerment of the company or its people.

But should we reward a research team that fails for the fourth time to find the solution to a nagging problem - on the way to a new product? What if those failures are commonplace? Where do we draw the line? Edison tried a thousand types of material before finding tungsten for the core of the light bulb. If he had been a research employee reporting to you, at what point would you have pulled the plug on the project, or become disillusioned with the person?

The culture of the company you grow is very much influenced by your actions in rewarding or punishing employees or whole departments. And the best companies seem to be those that are motivated from the top to push limits within reason in order to find better ways to do things, to create products, to expand the market. The CEO must realize that most such efforts lead to a dead end or will fail outright.

I was once in the record business. Speak about insanity. Only two percent of all records released broke even. Of course, the major hits paid for thousands of misses. In venture capital, the conventional wisdom is that one in ten investments will more than pay for the complete loss of half of those ten investments. Yet investors reward the VC's with a track record of one in ten, and record companies still churn out a reduced number of recordings, knowing that a great majority will fail to break even.

So, where does the learned, best of breed CEO step in to administer punishment? As the headline infers, a visionary, proactive leader should not be able to stand by and condone inaction. That is not only a waste of corporate assets, but the fixed overhead eaten by the inactive period keeps draining the cash and time resources of the corporation with nothing to show for it. Wouldn't you rather dissect a failure and move forward, than have nothing to show for time and money spent in wasted fixed overhead?

The coffee and wine school of innovation.
By Dave Berkus

Here's one for debate around a cup of coffee or a glass of wine. Most innovation occurs when creative people are relaxed and thinking about other things.

We all can picture the corporate R&D lab with tens of scientists working at white boards, or over computer models, or with prototypes. And we picture programmers working at their workstations or on their portable notebooks creating great new code.

But all of those people are following the flash of inspiration that started their activity, and it is that flash we seek to reproduce again and again in a successful enterprise.

This leads us back to coffee and wine, and showers, and quiet time. Given that we are looking for that flash of inspiration that starts us down the path of innovation through the hard work of R&D, maybe we should reengineer our thinking about allocation of time for our most creative resources, including ourselves.

There are times when creativity comes under pressure. Necessity, after all, is the mother of invention. But whole leaps into new groundbreaking areas of innovation most often come from times of reflection, when the mind is clear to dream ahead, to think without interruption.

So there are those who subscribe to the coffee and wine school, and encourage creative thinkers to find extra time in the early mornings or evenings to free the mind to innovate, to find the spark that could propel a company forward.

Protect your international traveling employees.
By Dave Berkus

As your company grows, you will probably have to make conclusions about traveling employees, and travel for yourself. There are vast opportunities internationally that require careful planning to execute well. One of the most critical decisions is how to enter a new country or region. Most companies early in to the process do not have the resources to place people on the ground in foreign countries, so they make new relationships with distributors or dealers to represent them in the new areas.

As you begin your travels into new territories away from home, it is always wise to have a host to greet you from arrival through departure in each country that is new to you. If you do not yet have any firm relationships in a country, develop some connection using your outreach channels before the first flight. Even if you are going to start a series of interviews, you can have one candidate meet you at the airport and another later return you to the airport. You should find this connection occurs automatically later as the relationships mature and you have either dealers or your own personnel within each territory.

The customs, laws and even the knowledge of safety dos and don'ts are critical elements in assuring your safety and that of your traveling employees. It is also good business to learn local customs from locals. Having a local contact to provide information to your home and your work is a relief to all, including yourself.

Then there is the question of creation of a regional office to cover multiple countries in a geographic area. It is the next logical step toward creating corporate entities abroad. And the regional manager hired to oversee multiple countries can act as country manager for his or her home country, often volunteering to travel with you to the various countries in the region. That's the best and safest choice for a next step toward becoming a true, international entity with offices in numerous countries as you grow.

Money motivates.

By Dave Berkus

Salaries or hourly wages must be within reasonable limits set by the industry and matched by the competition, both regionally and for the same job classification. But more difficult is the sticky issue of employee incentive compensation. I find that this is an area much more often the subject of a CEO phone call, a roundtable discussion, or a board compensation committee meeting.

There are many studies that can tell us how various industries reward employees for achievement above a base pay, or beyond expectation. And there are some industries where tools such as stock options are considered mandatory for a company to be competitive. But how about listing the basics for designing an excellent incentive compensation program? Here are several, gleaned from numerous companies and systems of compensation.

First, *be rule specific.* A bonus or commission that is granted after the fact, without a target plan or without objectives to meet, is surely appreciated, but does not often create an incentive to exceed, only an expectation of receipt again in the next period. When a leader and a subordinate agree upon a list of achievements in advance, then good performance can be rewarded based upon a fair assessment of accomplishments against those achievements. And if those goals are aligned with those of the overall corporation, everyone wins and the process can be repeated in subsequent periods.

Second, there should be a substantial carrot, or *upside bonus for outstanding achievement.* A sales commission plan should reward a salesperson with a combination of salary and commission up to the expected level of performance, often called a quota. Perhaps a part of that compensation plan should include a bonus upon achievement of quota, as a form of recognition and celebration. Then, contrary to popular thinking, there should be an increasing reward for achievement above the expected number, beyond the list of agreed-upon incentives for non-commissioned employees. For a salesperson, the commission percentage should increase above quota, and a second level of bonus available at some higher point. Sometimes, a combination of revenue, gross profit and even operating income form the basis for individual and team rewards.

Next, some form of rewards should be designed to *be immediate*. Rewarding a February achievement in December disconnects the reward from the event, reducing the effect of the reward itself. If we believe that money does motivate, then we should reward positive behavior immediately to reinforce that behavior.

Finally, and perhaps most difficult to design, there must be *protection against workarounds* or from employees gaming the system. Reward only gross revenues, and salespeople will push the limit of profitability, impacting the corporation but not their commissions. Real estate agents are paid as a percentage of the sale, not upon its relationship to the asking price. Sometimes, agents push their clients to accept low offers to assure a quick closing of a deal, since their participation percentage is only slightly affected by a price cut to close the deal quickly.

There are more insidious ways to game a compensation system. Wall Street brokers helped to create the financial crisis by following a bonus system driven by quantity, not quality of trades. Salespeople paid entirely upon closing a deal will care less about the subsequent completion of a complex, time-consuming transaction. Support people paid based upon the number of tickets closed will rush to close tickets at the expense of quality service. There must be thousands of such examples where poorly designed systems allow employees to achieve personal goals that are at odds with the best interest of the corporation or its customers.

So use these four items as a checklist as you create compensation plans for various levels and types of employees. *Rule specific; substantial upside bonus; immediate rewards; protection against working around the system.*

Chapter Five. GROWTH!

By far the most enjoyable part of building a business of any size is experiencing the thrill of growth. And although "a rising tide lifts all boats" helping many businesses to grow without as much effort, there certainly are methods, strategies and tools to aid in growing the enterprise regardless of the trends.

In this chapter, we explore insights dealing with trends, recurring and incremental revenues, methods of measurement and control, and issues dealing with resources required to support growth.

But there are so many ways your effort toward your goal can be sideswiped or frustrated from the inside and from the outside. We will explore issues that are most important strategically to you, your board and your managers. Business cycles are a fact of life, and those of us who have lived through many cycles have gained experience in finding the proper time to step on the gas and when to use the brakes.

We'll explore these and much more.

Fish in the giant ocean - not in a shallow creek.

By Dave Berkus

This is like a Hans Christian Anderson parable, but aimed at you and your business... There are big fish and small fish, potential customers, all swimming in the sea that is your potential marketplace. You, the lonely fisherman, have to weave a net to catch your fish. Should your net be large and bulky, requiring more effort and expense to weave? Or should it be small and delicate, to catch those fish that would otherwise fall through the net?

The size of your market may well define the ultimate size of your dream. You can be the most successful coffee house owner in a city of ten thousand, or the founding CEO of the largest chain of coffee shops on the continent. Defining your market in a limiting way reduces the opportunity to exploit the larger potential that may be available to you.

If you attempt to create a manufacturing business where the total available market for your products is only $30 million, even success leading to a dominant share of the market would not allow your company to scale it to a size of great interest to investors.

This lesson is important. Companies grow proportional to the size of the market, and success cannot turn a limited market opportunity into a grand enterprise.

When we investors look at a business plan, we look immediately to see if there is research to support the claim of a large enough market to expect the candidate company to grow into the size projected. And we look to see if the size projected is large enough to interest us as investors, since that is directly proportional to the ultimate value of the company in a liquidity event.

To the point of the headline above, sometimes an entrepreneur claims that there is a large market, and attempts to make the case for growth into a grand scale company, sharing only a relatively small portion of that market. If the market claimed to be of a large size has no current, fast growing competitors, we must guess at the accuracy of the claim – something very unscientific. But if there are entrants already scaling, often we then can focus upon the differences and advantages our candidate entrepreneur brings to the market, a much more comfortable piece of work for the investors.

The size of your dream must be scaled to fit into the size of your marketplace. Be sure you can back up your claim with some form of research, then work to perfect the differentiation you offer against the competition.

And if your market truly is large but of unknown size, and if there are no competitors growing in the market, you must work doubly hard to convince investors of your dream. Yet, there are wonderful cases where entrepreneurs created and grew vast enterprises in new markets which could not be measured when their journey began. Think of FedEx, AOL, Microsoft, Cisco Systems, Facebook, YouTube, and tens of other billion dollar or larger players in markets that did not exist or were in their infancy when those entrepreneurs cast their nets.

Back to basics: Make your financials work for you.

By JJ Richa

How many units (widgets or hours) do you need to sell - and for what price - to be profitable? It's a simple question that sometimes takes us deeply into the murky waters of accounting detail. Yet, many companies have made huge mistakes when failing to properly calculate break-even for products and services. A break-even analysis is a very useful tool that can help you understand the sources of profit in your business.

A break-even analysis is a tool to determine the sales level at which the business is neither incurring a loss nor making a profit. In other words, the break-even point for a business is when the total expenses equal total revenue. To analyze break-even, you need to divide your income statement into three, not two sections, breaking out variable costs from fixed costs. So we will call it the *profit and loss management statement* instead.

In order to develop your profit and loss management statement, you need to do further analysis of your expenses, by accurately classifying them as either fixed costs or variable costs.

Fixed costs are those expenses that generally do not change in the short term regardless of how much you sell. Examples of fixed costs include general office expenses, rent, depreciation, most salaries, utilities, telephone, property tax, insurance and the like.

Variable costs are those expenses that change with the level of sales. These costs vary with sales because they are directly involved in making the sale. Examples of variable costs include direct materials, direct labor, cost of goods sold, sales commissions, freight, royalties, and the like.

Looking at your income statement, review the current classification of which expenses are fixed and which are variable. If a sale creates an associated expense, it's a variable cost. If a cost can go either way (fixed or variable), try to determine what portion of the cost is fixed and what portion of the cost is variable, otherwise consider it fixed. It may be helpful to ask yourself the following question: If the business did not sell any product or service, would it still have to pay a specific expense? If the answer is yes, that item is a fixed cost.

Most accounting systems will allow you to reclassify an account between fixed and variable expense and automatically move all transactions without disturbing the net profit.

Knowing your total sales, total variable costs and total fixed costs allows you to determine your *contribution margin* - basically the remainders after your variable costs are taken into consideration. Calculate your variable costs as a percentage of sales - and your contribution margin becomes the remaining percentage that would contribute to covering all other costs – the fixed costs. To obtain your break-even, you can divide the fixed costs by the contribution margin percentage.

If your fixed costs are not covered, there will be no profit. Losses will probably continue. You should fix what's broken in your business, provide for investment to cover expected losses until break-even, or halt operations to avoid draining all remaining resources. If your variable costs are not covered, you are in the wrong business, since you are selling your product or service for less than what it would cost you to produce such product or service.

One of the ways to be profitable is for you to know your break-even cost, sometimes call it your "nut," and set a goal for profits. Without having a goal, there is little chance for reaching your potential. Knowing the unit cost of a product or a service, you can determine how many units (widgets or hours) must be sold in order to reach break-even or a proposed profit level. This may be basic, but profit is the ultimate goal and measure of operating business success.

Execute the plan - or execute the planner.
By Dave Berkus

It is all about execution. Waiting over a year to see results is too long, since your chance of mid-course correction is greatly reduced. To make the point, Harvard's Robert Kaplan believes that less than 10% of corporate strategies are effectively executed. Ouch!

If that is true, we are tolerant bunch. We carefully plan in long, dedicated sessions each year of so, then draw up a series of goals, strategies, tactics, objectives, targets, or whatever we want to name them. We hold all-company meetings where possible, and departmental meetings to roll out the new plan.

We set individual objectives and rewards to match these goals. Then we manage day-to-day routine execution, and periodically measure the results. Sound familiar? This is the description of a well-managed process within what should be a well-managed company.

And yet, Kaplan is close to right, whether it's 10% or 30%, it is a minority of strategies that are effectively executed. Why? Here is a list to use as a guide to better execution.

Make the plan simple to understand. Once deployed down one or more levels in the organization, like the old game of telephone, the corporate plan begins to look less like the original as each department attempts to adopt it and create departmental objectives to conform. A complex plan stacks the deck against all but those who created it at the top.

Put someone in charge of executing the plan. That may be you, but in some companies, that requires a dedicated individual tasked with removing roadblocks, measuring success, and reporting progress.

Provide feedback loops at each critical stage of execution. If the plan calls for increased revenues, measure output and efficiency as well as revenues. Look for leading, not lagging indicators of change.

Make sure you provide the resources necessary to hit the plan, including money, new hire authorizations, and above all, clear instruction and delegation form the top.

Listen to complaints, suggestions and warning signs. Respond, so that people know you are serious about execution of the plan. Modify what is not working. Then pivot, when necessary, to scrap part of the plan, and then rewrite it in order to meet its objectives.

If a plan has realistic goals and if you are reasonably able to provide the resources necessary to complete the plan successfully, you are way ahead of that other 90%.

But if you toss a plan out to others to execute, don't follow through until the end, fail to measure, or to provide needed resources, then you will deserve your fate. So take heed. If you go to the effort to plan, go to the effort to succeed.

Premature scaling kills businesses.
By Dave Berkus

Venture capitalists sometimes make an error in directing their portfolio company CEOs to push resources to the limit and scale the business to immense size quickly, all to seize market share. The logic in this is simple: once a company has market share, other issues can be sorted out to monetize the market, make the company profitable, scoop up wavering competitors, or even sell the company to a larger firm looking for a large customer base.

This form of thinking has been unusually true during the rise of social media, where market share became the primary goal of a company, with revenues and profitability to follow later. It was true for Amazon and other visionary companies that grabbed market share during the early Internet era. But beware. Many, many companies accepting venture capital lost it all following this instruction. VCs have a goal of creating extraordinary value for their investors. Incremental profits from companies that later sell for three to five times their original value at the time of their investment may be considered great successes for founders but relative failures for VCs, who must hit for the fences with every early stage investment.

I've been involved as a board member of two such businesses, where venture investors came aboard and pushed management to immediately scale the business without regard for profitability, and without much regard for infrastructure. Both businesses scaled beyond what their market could absorb, and revenues did not build at nearly the rate of audience increase. The cost of each exercise was dramatic, far beyond what a founder-entrepreneur would order to be spent when using his or her capital or reinvesting cash flow from operations. Venture investors need large scale to make large exit valuations, or in many cases are not interested in maintaining marginal companies. To state it again, what might be a success to angel investors and to founders could be only of marginal interest to a typical VC.

Scaling a business is an art as well as a science. By definition, scaling requires the addition of fixed overhead, sometimes the kind you cannot shed easily, including leases for expanded space. Experienced CEOs often make it a habit to scale as a result of demand, reducing risk and mating cost to growth in revenues. Angel investors are more tolerant of this than VCs. Typically, when you bring a VC onboard, you increase the risk, the reward, and the definition of the size for a successful exit. Adding to this is the extra risk undertaken by premature scaling. It is important for you to realize that there is a fair tradeoff in valuation between a company with less outside investment and a lower endgame sales price, and one that shoots for a much higher valuation to justify a higher amount of outside investment.

Nail it; then scale it.
By Dave Berkus

So your business has begun to take off. You've figured out your channels of distribution, pricing model and how to support your growing list of customers. Don't be alarmed by this next statement. *That's relatively easy.*

You can be the one to develop a product or service, promote it, and support it when you are a small operation. But what if you need to repeat the process of positioning, selling, and supporting your product ten thousand or more times as often as you do today?

It's worth repeating my *every three million dollar crisis* insight. You will have recurring crises as you grow your business. These are predictable and usually arrive in the same recurring order, and often with every $3 million in additional annual gross profit from revenues as you grow.

The first crisis is financial, funding the business, development, inventory, and marketing. The second crisis is organizational. At about the twenty employee level, the organization is too large for one person to handle internal operations, and a new level of management must be inserted between the founder and the existing team, causing communication and control issues that many founders have not experienced.

The third crisis is one of quality control. At about $6 million in revenue, there are so many new customers that product or service quality is stretched to the limit, and complaints about quality surface in quantities you never experienced previously.

Guess what? And, at about $9 million in annual revenue, the cycle repeats, with financial needs for additional working capital and money for growth churning to the top of the problem stack. And, as you grow, the same class of problems returns but with a larger scale and more urgent cry for attention - and more ruinous if not solved.

It is important - no it is urgent - that you solve these problems and know how to spot them coming in advance. To scale any company to a large size, you must know how to solve the problems of production, customer service, working capital needs and more in order to keep the company on the rails. The cost in lost efficiency, customer referrals, and corporate reputation is too high not to make this a priority for a growing business.

Many of the insights in this book and the BERKONOMICS series deal with the issues of scaling your business. As you feel more and more comfortable being able to scale each portion of the operation, you will be able to focus upon other areas of weakness, spreading the risk out and into a manageable range, rather than overwhelming you and your growing staff with their magnitude.

But wherever possible, it is best to nail down the processes and structure before and as you scale the business, not in emergency response to issues as they develop and grow to threaten the enterprise.

Drive your recurring revenues.
By David Steakley

I have a positive fetish for recurring revenue. When I hear a company pitch a business model which I believe has the potential to acquire a customer once, and keep the customer paying for a multi-year period without further marketing expense, my ears perk up. Typical examples are software as a service (SaaS) models, or any kind of content-driven subscription model.

There are so many things to love about a company with this kind of subscription model. Especially for a provider of a virtual good or service, costs of goods sold do not scale with sales, as they do in the real world. In the virtual world, a much higher percentage of incremental revenue falls straight to the bottom line. In most businesses, you can look at the revenues all you want, and you can draw pretty pictures extrapolating the curve of revenue growth, but, usually, the reality is, the company needs to go out and sell the annual revenue all over again every single year.

With the right recurring revenue model, top line growth can really shoot the lights out. Each year, the company can commence with a reasonably predictable big portion of last year's revenues already in the bag.

It requires special capabilities and expertise to really capitalize on a recurring revenue model, and a different way of measuring success for both executives and investors. Subscription businesses typically take longer to get to profitability, because costs of developing the product or service, and customer acquisition costs, are front-loaded, while revenue is back-loaded. By conventional measures of company performance, a recurring revenue company can appear to be struggling at first, but you have to know what measures are predictive for this kind of company.

The key calculation is the cost of customer acquisition, compared to the gross margin contribution of the customer. If an analysis of the gross margin on a new customer acquisition reveals that customer acquisition costs can be recouped in two years, you're doing well. If you get back customer acquisition costs in one year, you're doing *great*. This assumes reasonably low churn of 10% or less.

The crucial turning-point for a recurring revenue model with a potentially massive market is the moment when the acquisition model is sufficiently effective, refined, and repeatable, so you can blow it out and scale it up. If you've got a favorable payback period for customer acquisition, and you can repeatedly perform the acquisition model, then that is the moment to forget about profitability and spend like a crazy person by scaling up the sales machine.

When you go to sell the company, you'll get paid based on the slope of the recurring revenue curve (up and to the right), and even if a company sale is not in your plan, you'll be glad you sacrificed current profitability for the longer term, if you've picked the right moment to go big.

I've always thought Steve Case was the early genius of this kind of thinking. In the late 90s, you could had a hard time picking up your mail without finding an AOL software connection CD in the mailbox. AOL spent about $300 million sending out those CDs, and at one point, half the world's production of CDs had the AOL logo on them. The lifetime value of an AOL subscriber was about $350. Average customer acquisition cost was about $35. That extreme in postal spamming took AOL from an IPO market value of $70 million to a merger value of $150 billion when the combined with Time Warner. Wow.

Recurring revenue companies have been changing hands in the last few years at four to six times' annual recurring revenue. Steve Case's Time-Warner bonanza of perfect timing may not be repeated any time soon, but the appetite for these kinds of companies is more robust than ever.

My story: Fail locally, one customer at a time.
By Frank Peters

We've all heard the modern day mantra: *Fail Fast*. It's good advice; the theory being that entrepreneurs can discover the flaws in their business models sooner, make course corrections and move in a more favorable direction.

In my case as a young software entrepreneur, I had a different approach: *Fail Locally, one customer at a time*. Perhaps like many businesses, mine started out painfully slow; wage-wise, I think it was three years before I earned $30,000. For me I had few alternatives; working for someone else had proved to be a frustrating experience. I became an entrepreneur by default. I was fortunate that I could write software and doubly fortunate that my despair at working for 'the Man' -

and feeling compelled to strike out on my own - coincided with the dawn of the personal computer era.

I've often looked back and said that you didn't have to be a genius at that time. You just had to be lucky, write reasonably good code and land in an industry with some legs, and of course, treat the customer well. Prior to bombing out of corporate life, I worked as a management consultant and at a very early age I was dealing with the presidents of very large companies. This would serve me very well as my product moved from individual clients to entire Wall Street firms licensing my code. But there was something else at work here.

I can't imagine encouraging an entrepreneur to follow in my path, but for me, operating alone with no board of advisors, no business plan and no outside capital, I was making it up as I went. I look back and describe the early days as 'selling software out of the trunk of my car'. I would write code all night then get in the car around noon each day to make my rounds. On the West Coast, where I started, the stock market closed at 1pm and that's when my customers wanted to see me.

I was fortunate that these individual customers were well healed; they had the money and were looking for an excuse to buy a computer. As I look back, I can remember so many times where I benefited from good luck. Who would've guessed that a day would come when a major Wall Street firm would make a strategic decision to open high profile offices across Southern California? How would they populate these new fancy offices? They would lure the best and the brightest away from their current employers with fat cash advances – enough for a new car, and a new computer. I was a beneficiary of this development. When one of my clients was recruited away from a user, and all his new officemates saw his computer, pretty soon I was invited into the new companies for all those 'me, too' sales.

Oh, how I tortured these early clients! Ours was a 2-man operation in those earliest of days; I knew nothing of quality assurance. It would not be unlikely at all that a major update to the software would break critical features that previously worked fine. Flaws like these could cripple my clients, causing them grief, lost productivity and worse, a loss of good will with their clients. Thankfully, these mini disasters occurred in small sizes. I could fix the bugs and hand-deliver the repairs before I infected more clients. In this way I learned a great deal. I would take the slings and arrows of my disappointed clients face to face. And I would learn customer service.

Years later, when news of my product spread to Wall Street and I had my first appointments in these corporate offices, I was well prepared. My earliest job experiences had placed me in similar hallowed places; I was not overwhelmed. At this point in the company's life, I had developed a mature product used by thousands of happy individual clients who were clamoring for the home office to build interfaces to minimize their manual data entry. But maybe best of all, as we arrived in Manhattan to move my officer to the source, I arrived with a good reputation and, as I like to say, I hadn't pissed off anybody on Wall Street.

From this point the company grew like wild fire. People liked the product and by buying a license for everyone in their firms, these Wall Street executives were rewarding their hard working sale force. It was hard to believe, but this was a new concept back in the days of 'green screens' that only offered market pricing data to the people who made all the money for the firm. We became as popular as the *hoola hoop*. We went from our largest-ever sale of 3 licenses at one time to a thousand. In ninety days we sold three major firms; and this would only be the beginning of our rapid growth. I look back today and muse, "No one ever asked us if we could deliver all that software." And oh, did we struggle as we learned all over again how to provide customer service to these large and demanding new clients.

Could an entrepreneur follow this same business model today? I suppose that's what limited releases are all about. But in our case, our test clients consumed us for our first nine years of existence – no one would advise a similar strategy today. We were lucky that we were able to learn so many painful lessons on a small and local scale. By the time a large opportunity came along, we were ready.

The five kinds of risk in building your business
By Dave Berkus

If you could predict a crisis within your business before its occurrence, wouldn't you move to prevent or reduce its impact? Making such predictions is a skill that can be developed, and here's one method of doing so.

There are five basic kinds of internal risks than a business faces over time. Of course, there are external risks that cannot be controlled or predicted, but can be planned for as well – natural disasters, sudden political or economic events that rattle the entire economy, and more. That discussion is for a future time. Here are risks you can address.

First, there is *market risk*. Will the marketplace accept your product? Is there a market for your class of product at all? Market risk is constant and should be of greatest concern to any executive or entrepreneur. Mitigating market risk is not easy. Someone within your firm must be finely attuned to the changes in the market, including subtle signs from competitors. If you are big enough to have a dedicated product manager, that person is a good candidate for this ongoing task, as is a marketing manager, who should be attuned to the changes in the environment.

Second is *product risk*. Totally controllable within your organization, the quality and durability of your finished product should be at the top of someone's job description. Whether it is you or a quality control manager, someone must assure that the product or service you send out to the world will not fail to perform at least to the level of customer expectation, if not to delight those customers most likely to be critical.

Third is *finance risk*. Too often the person you call your chief financial officer is trained in accounting, which is primarily a process of looking backward over events in the past. A real CFO must be one to project and plan for the future as well, aware of the need for increased cash during times of growth or market disruption, and aware of the weekly challenges of shifting cash flow. The worst thing a fragile, entrepreneurial business can endure is to run out of cash. Not only is the enterprise threatened, but confidence is shaken among employees, suppliers, even customers. Competitors have a field day when hearing about cash problems at a company; and the rumors they pass on can reverberate for months or longer after the problem is solved.

Fourth is *competitive risk*, which consists of two separate risks. Do you have a significant barrier to entry to keep competitors from undermining your effort? And does a competitor have a better story and product to compete effectively against your offering? Someone within your firm must be finely attuned to the changes in the subtle signs from competitors. These include having a current knowledge of competitors' hiring practices, pricing strategy, and more.

It is your job to oversee the constant gathering of information, efforts to mitigate these risks, and even to hold senior level planning meetings around analyzing data and asking "what if…" questions that bring out the doomsday scenarios that could hobble your company. Once defined, the obvious next step is to role play responses to each challenge, or even to put in place preventative measures well in advance for each identified risk.

When one or several of these events hit you and your team, and they certainly will someday, you'll be better prepared to respond quickly and with a more appropriate, planned response. That will reduce the possibilities of suffering a catastrophe, and will more quickly calm the many stakeholders who have reason for concern, looking to you for assurances.

Why not plan a series of meetings with the appropriate members of your firm to discuss these challenges as you and they identify them, and prepare a plan for overcoming each? The time it takes may well be the difference between survival and doom; or it may be the plan that distances you from your competition if events do occur in your mutual future.

White-label it: Make it 'YOU' inside.
By David Steakley

Companies can strike it rich by finding an element of business operations which many companies need, but few have the capability or expertise to execute with excellence – and then aim to supply that element. Sometimes this is called a *white label* strategy, because your customers offer your product as their own product, writing in their brand name on the blank label in your underlying offering.

But, more often, this is just the virtualization of what we used to call outsourcing. On the web, not only does no one know much of who you are, but no one cares how you sourced your widgets.

Bazaarvoice, a company in Austin, Texas is a great example of this kind of operation. To be quite frank, the first two or three times someone told me what they do, I couldn't understand it. My preconceived notions of the possible range of business models simply didn't include this one.

Basically, the company created software for online forums. Really, that's a business? Yep: revenues of over $100 million per year with a market cap around $800 million. The company identified an element of operations which almost every online retailer already has, or needs, but very few do well on their own. Moreover, the company's offerings allow the retailer to change a thing which may be seen as mostly a pain - into an engine for increasing sales, for sharpening the retailer's value proposition, for catching and solving problems before they become real problems. In short, the underlying value of that company is the old-fashioned underlying value of outsourcing (if there was one): *the outsourcer not only does it for you, the outsourcer shows you how to do it right, and does it at lower cost.*

Now listen to one of Bazaarvoice's short pitches: "Our industry-leading social commerce solutions capture & amplify user-generated content, driving the highest social media ROI, for the world's largest brands." Forgive me, but I had no idea what that meant.

I heard another pitch recently, for a company which must have been unknowingly inspired by that other obscure pitch. This one wants to supply product comparison mechanisms for online merchants. You know, those bubble charts of products and features, by model? Do you want zoom in your camera? How much zoom? How many pixels? Thank god I had finally grasped Bazaarvoice; otherwise I probably would have sent these guys packing.

There's a lesson in this for business operators. Look around your operations, and identify areas of cost which, as far as you can tell, do little or nothing to enhance the profitability of your operations - but, you must have them. Can someone do it better than you, and at lower cost? Have an open mind. You're used to outsourcing payroll, bookkeeping, and logistics. Just for an exercise, see if you can identify someone to outsource absolutely everything in your business.

You have only so much management bandwidth. It can only make you more effective - if you're able to focus your attention on the things you're best at doing – your core competency.

Back to basics: Better manage your cash flow.
By JJ Richa

"Cash is King." You've heard this so many times it sounds trite. But in *trite* often is *truth*.

Without sufficient cash, even the most profitable business ceases to exist. Cash flow is not about profitability; it is about timing - timing of cash flowing in and out of the business. No matter how much you sell, if you don't collect the money, you're going to go out of business. As business owners, we often get so wrapped up in selling our products and services that we forget to take the time to ensure we're managing our cash flow and receiving the money for those sales.

It is simply insufficient to focus only upon total sales dollars. It is as important to focus on the cash collection of those sales. Reacting to cash flow problems instead of planning ahead means you are already in a bad position. It is imperative to take proactive measures to stay on top of your cash flow and improve the bottom line. Here are some tips:

1. **Know your business' balance sheet.** Many owners focus on the business' profit and loss statement alone. It's a potentially fatal mistake because healthy profits can mask an impending cash flow crisis. You need a structured balance sheet that includes all the influencing factors including debts, interest payments, inventory, with special attention to "current assets" and "current liabilities" – those due within one year.

2. **Cash Flow Statement and Cash Flow Projection.** Many business people don't know how cash flow works and its significance to keeping their operation afloat. There are several different cash flow reports available from your accounting system. A cash flow statement shows you how much cash is going into and out of your business. A cash flow projection is a forward looking report that estimates your future cash needs. Be aware of when you expect lean cash flow patches coming up and plan accordingly. Avoid funding major purchases from your business' working capital unless you are sure you have the cash to cover it. (In *BERKONOMICS* lingo, Dave states emphatically: "Never use short term cash to pay long term debt or buy new major assets.")

3. **Require upfront payment on projects.** The upfront payment may be a down payment, a percentage of the full project, a full payment for capital equipment, or any combination so that your customers fund the project, not you.

4. **Set your terms to be due in full upon completion.** Get your money as soon as you can and if you can avoid standard 30 day terms, it would be better yet. Certainly don't extend beyond 30 days after you've completed your work. Offer small discounts for early payment as an incentive.

5. **Negotiate terms with your vendors.** Take advantage of credit terms and prioritize payments according to the consequences involved in becoming overdue. Ideally you want to extend your payment for 30

days or more. This will give you the opportunity to complete the work, bill and receive payments from your customers prior to paying vendors. Wages, taxes and direct debits must be paid on-time. Key suppliers may be prepared to wait, just to keep your business. Don't pay early just to get a discounted price unless the discount is better than being without cash.

6. **Implement a collection process.** Follow through when your customers delay payments because they're using your cash. Be diligent about collecting from your customers. Stay in close touch with major debtors as payment deadlines approach. This requires continuous surveillance, and often is missed by small businesses with limited time and resources – a mistake.

7. **Set up a line of credit.** Obtaining a line of credit from your bank for an emergency reserve is a smart move, since lending rates are for the most part less than the late fees your vendors charge. And you know the old adage: the best time to get money is when you don't need it.

8. **Use available finance products.** Overdrafts, premium funding, lease facilities, even business credit cards and cash flow funding products can all be good tools to help ease the squeeze. *Factoring* or *asset based financing / lending* allows you to sell your receivables for cash now, in lieu of waiting for customers to pay. Associated fees may be high, so it is imperative to ensure that the benefits exceed the cost of waiting for customers' payments.

9. **Owner draws.** Each dollar you take from your company reduces the amount of cash flow you'll have available for the business to grow. Minimize owner's draws and try to depend on a fixed salary.

10. **Taxes and Penalties.** Avoid incurring unexpected taxes and statutory penalties. This may require help from your accountant or CFO to schedule due dates for all taxes on a calendar. You may want to eliminate all payroll tax risk by outsourcing your payroll to a vendor that "impresses" the taxes for you. An important side effect of good tax planning is to save yourself the money and the stress.

It is worth repeating: the best time to seek money is when you don't need it. No one wants to provide cash to a business that is experiencing cash flow problems. All cash is not created equal and you should consider timing, amount, usage, cost, control issues and consequences.

Create your budget from the top. Plan downward.

By Dave Berkus

Many people believe that bottom up budgeting leads to waste and misdirection. The advocates of top-down budgeting are strong in their belief that if you give each person or department no guidance, they will budget to their wants or specific needs, not to those that support a corporate goal.

So, they argue: Give your people a top-down generated target. Have them fit their plans into the target. This way the corporate financial and strategic goals come from the top, as they should, and all departments fit into those strategies with their contribution and their overhead.

Over many years, in in many companies, I've overseen budgeting both ways, and agree with the advocates that it is often masked waste in the form of allowances for unknowns, extra padding for protection, and even higher budgeted expense numbers to make the managers look good at the end of year by under-spending, that are found deep within bottom-up budgets.

On the other hand, often departments cannot fit their required costs into the structure required to meet a profit goal for the corporation, or just as important, corporate revenue goals. In both instances, top down or bottom up, negotiations between department and corporate managers require compromise. The difference is that in a top down budget, the discussion almost always centers on compromises to meet the corporate goal, a much more important discussion than one centered around department goals.

Budgeting from the bottom up more often works in non-profit enterprises, where many departments are involved deeply into the detail of staffing and program delivery, and where the goal of the non-profit is service, not profit.   Either way, a budget is a necessary road map for a successful enterprise, and should never be ignored or worked upon after the year is already underway.

Whatever it is, try to deliver it via the cloud.
By David Steakley

Everyone knows that software-as-a-service has displaced the old style of delivering enterprise software. You may have assumed that this has transpired as a natural evolution of technological capabilities. Wrong. The key driver is to shorten the decision path.

With old-school enterprise software, closing a sale required you to get the customer's lawyers to sign off on the software license; getting the customer's IT personnel to bless your architecture and grudgingly deign to allow your software to enter the holy chambers of IT; getting the green shades to issue a check which would often contain six figures or more; persuading the IT gnomes to buy adequate disk space, CPU power, terminals, and network capacity to allow your software to operate; and many other relatively impossible hurdles. It is kind of amazing, in retrospect, that any enterprise software was ever purchased.

Software-as-a-service, often sold in a *freemium* model with the simple features available at no cost, allows the individual end user to decide on a whim to try out your solution, and IT never even has to know! "Contract? Well, there was some funny language I clicked on..."

There's a lesson in this for any company which intends to try to sell to huge corporations: design a sales model which requires the least possible action by the customer in order to close the sale, that involves the least number of corporate personnel, and requires the smallest possible amount of cash outlay at the outset. The closer you can be to allowing the actual end user of your product or service to decide on his or her own to buy your product or service, the better off you are.

If this type of approach simply doesn't work for what you're doing, then you have to grit your teeth and plan for success, to overcome the inherent obstacles of selling to corporations.

There's gold in repurposing intellectual property.
By Dave Berkus

Several times a month, I'd have lunch with one of my CEOs, and each time we'd find ourselves digging into the intellectual property developed by the company over the years, just to refresh ourselves about what the intended use was back then, and whether new developments or technologies might make these older ideas and patents relevant again.

Since I have been involved at the board level with so many companies over the years, sometimes I can see connections that might be missed by a CEO with a singular focus. So I was surprised and excited when one of these verbal fishing expeditions during a lunch brought up a technology the company had patented back in 1995 and forgotten. The Internet was young, and the patented product allowed a visitor to dial into a computer (does anyone remember dial-up electronic bulletin boards?) and be redirected to a screen that would allow the user to identify himself, pay any fees required for use and agree to the terms of service.

From my more recent experience, I recognized that this describes exactly what every guest must do when attempting to gain access to the Internet in a hotel, or Starbucks, or any of thousands of public places. And I recalled that there was a patent war starting to take shape in this segment, centered about who was first to patent just this guest access.

It turns out that our patent was years ahead of those others, and was general enough to cover all forms of access to the Internet, not just dial up. The CEO began what continues as a licensing effort and lawsuits to protect the patent that could be worth more money in the end than the entire corporation was worth before the discovery.

Intellectual property is the principle asset of technology companies. The value of old patents cannot be easily estimated as new technologies reinvigorate those patents for new uses, such as the one we discovered during lunch. So: do you have hidden treasure in your vault?

Patent litigation can kill the small guy.
By Dave Berkus

When you think of patents, you think of added value to the corporation in the form of protection of its intellectual property. In fact, many corporations spend millions developing surrounding patents to form what is known as a "patent thicket," much like Brer Rabbit jumped into to protect himself against his detractors in the briar patch. Investors like to see patents or patent applications as evidence of intellectual property value and barriers to entry.

But there is a darker side to patent protection. The cost for filing patents and extending the filings to multiple countries is expensive, but often manageable. The problems come from either prosecuting or defending a patent, and those problems can come in many forms.

First, if your patent is challenged at any point, even after it has been granted, the cost of defense is dramatically higher than the original patent filing and attorney fees. It has become a common practice for large companies to fight their patent wars in the Patent Office itself, by filing legal challenges, requiring re-examination and sometimes an appeals process that can lead all the way to appeals court.

Second, if you elect to prosecute a violator of your patent, you begin a process you cannot easily abandon. Depending upon the size of the company or companies you go after, some will counter sue for violation of adjacent patents they may own, or sue for causes seemingly unrelated to the patent. This happened to one of my companies, and the cost of defense escalated out of control, exceeding the cost of prosecution, ultimately contributing to the death of the company.

Third, if you are sued in a patent case, and elect not to settle the suit early (bypassing a strategy of the prosecution), then your defense costs increase over time to reach amounts a small company CEO would never permit if in control of the situation. But to defend a lawsuit is not to control it. And patent litigation can kill the small guy.

Growth! I sat in my own safety net while weaving it.
By Berni Jubb

My First Startup...

...never started, nor did my fifth or sixth. My desire to run something stirred inside me early in life, but the first real entrepreneurial adventure finally took hold after a lot of failed experiments. Each one had a steep learning curve. And all were missing a key ingredient or two. One thing, though, that never bothers an entrepreneur is fear of the unknown.

The good thing was that I had a certain ability to see ahead of the obvious horizon so I could often find resources we didn't have, and grasp those issues we knew we didn't know about. It is not today's idea that makes the business a success, it is tomorrow's. It is not today's screw up that really messes up your business but the one yesterday that you didn't know about.

I digress for a moment with a business lesson direct from the hand of our mentor at the time, Mister Berkus himself. I was asked to explain my issue at a CEO round table for one of Dave's membership groups. The date of the round table happened to coincide with the clearing up of the remains of a nasty event that caused my company to teeter on the edge of bankruptcy. Of course it wasn't just one event that was the cause, as you might guess. It was mismanagement that caused the event - rapid growth and the simultaneous realization by our big vendors that we had grown faster than our ability to pay.

The notorious *credit crunch*, as Wikipedia puts it succinctly "is often caused by a sustained period of careless and inappropriate lending which results in losses for lending institutions and investors in debt when the loans turn sour and the full extent of bad debts becomes known." Ouch!

We thought we had a friendly banker as a lifeboat. But the creditors and our bank somehow realized our "growth problem" all at about the same time, and when we went to use our bank line of credit, the bank told us we had *blown it* and the line was withheld. Our suppliers had been careless lenders - and we had been careless borrowers of their credit. The bank just sent us ... condolences. We missed all the signals. And we were one of the *twenty-five fastest growing companies* in the INC.500 list at that time. Double ouch!

In three weeks of fast restructuring of our credit, tamping down our growth, reworking our marketing plan, repairing our inventories, calming down our vendors, working with our bigger customers (i.e. fixing everything), we saved the company, and the bank pitched in to support our new plan. The post mortem occurred at Dave's round table a month later. I will always remember Dave's observation when I smugly concluded with "we know how to deal with this kind of thing now." He snarled across the table with a knowing smile . . . something like "It won't be this Pink Elephant that will sit on you again." These days I always have an eagle eye out for unknown Pink, Purple or Magenta Elephants waiting to trample on something I haven't thought of or experienced yet.

But how do you see these things before they hit you? What kinds of detectors are available to avoid these things? You can't stop an entrepreneur from starting a new business or activity that is viewed as hopelessly stupid by detractors - and merely insane by close relatives. As an entrepreneur, you have a genetic problem. The bomb disposal guy in The Hurt Locker comes to mind.

Entrepreneurs often crash headlong into these nasty, often dangerous and sometimes exhilarating experiences. I posit that in fact entrepreneurs sometimes tempt fate to get off on the experience - tread close to the edge to keep the fire inside burning. They sometimes don't care; they are often reckless adventurers. Or as one of the richest guys in the world is quoted as saying, "A real entrepreneur is somebody who has no safety net underneath him."

The problem is that we weave that safety net even as we sit in it, making the job doubly difficult.

Double down!

By Dave Berkus

This piece of wisdom came from Jeff Bezos, founder & CEO of Amazon, during a board meeting for one of the companies where he sits as board member. Jeff asked the question "Is there anything big or small, which is working better than you expected? Is there anywhere we could double down?"

Bezos' point was that we spend a lot of time focusing on what's not working in Board meetings (especially during difficult times) and not enough time focusing on what is surpassing expectations and how we can "double down" on those areas. Often times the key levers in businesses are found in little things that are really outperforming, whether by intention or not.

Although the scale of those businesses Jeff Bezos works with is probably much larger than those we deal with, his question is intriguing for multiple reasons.

We worry over projections and fix our budgets to match, and then we manage to the revenue and costs of the budget. But what If we separate ourselves from that mindset long enough to search for and find sparks of success sometimes buried within our sales statistics. A geographic territory or singe product in a larger product line, or a service that was developed as an afterthought: do any show unusual signs of breaking out and becoming unanticipated successes?

Do we have the ability to change our thought process, alter our marketing focus, take resources from other areas if needed, and double down to back up potential winners in the making? Most of us would track the increased revenues, look at those in the light of total revenue progress, and monitor the actuals against the budget. A visionary like Jeff Bezos might pivot to make the rising star a centerpiece of our focus, quickly adding resources to support it, and seeing how far we could push it to make an unexpected success.

We all should have our antenna up looking for what's working, and where we should double down.   Surprise breakouts are rare and wonderful, to be supported immediately to the limits of our resources. That's the way small companies become big companies.   It's the way surprising new products and services emerge from the pack and create new market leaders.

Chapter Six. THE END GAME.

In this final chapter, we explore issues important to the CEO and entrepreneur coming closer to the end game, which can take the form of the sale of the company, or preparation for an initial public offering, either of which provides liquidity to investors, stakeholders and founders. Or perhaps the founder sells all or a portion of founder stock, finally realizing an equity reward for all the work and risk of the years past.

We explore issues relating to preparation for the end run, the deal itself. If the goal of starting a business is to ultimately create wealth, then planning for that event becomes an integral part of management strategy at some point, perhaps even back at the point of ignition or startup.

Or the end game can be of an entirely different experience. Statistically, fifty percent of all start-ups *fail* within five years of founding. What of those entrepreneurs? What of the lessons learned? We include insights that address this more emotional possibility of an end game, some in the words of entrepreneurs who've lived through it first-hand.

Look for your strategic buyer first.
By John Huston

While you are busy building your high growth venture, you may have occasionally thought about which large companies might be the ultimate buyer of your company – a buyer that could optimize your idea, customer base, and team. If you have professional angels or venture capitalists among your funding sources, you have probably been focused on your company's sale well before they wrote their first checks.

To simplify the obvious question, you should ask: "In whose hands does my company have the greatest value?" But remember that each potential acquirer should be evaluated in terms of both their *ability* and their *willingness* to make an acceptable offer for your company.

Assessing their *ability* is fairly straightforward, especially if you will only take an all-cash bid. You merely need to forecast the likelihood over the next few years they will have the financial resources to be the high bidder for your venture. For publicly traded potential acquirers, reviewing their public filings regarding previous acquisitions can be quite illuminating - especially finding information about whether they have borrowed to finance past company purchases. Many large companies have a preferred template from which their deal teams rarely stray.

Once you are comfortable with a potential acquirer's ability to make a winning bid for your company, then you only need to focus on how to increase their *willingness* to do so. Ideally each target company has a history of consistently making acquisitions with deal terms you would accept. This means they routinely acquire strategic assets and not just financial cash flow streams, paying a premium to do so.

Let's presume that you have identified three to five targeted bidders whose interest in acquiring your company you now need to heighten. How can you accomplish this?

The first step should be to honestly assess the allure your company might have to each targeted strategic acquirer. Then think about how your company's daily activities are enhancing that most attractive aspect of your business in the eyes of each potential bidder. This makes it much easier to allocate your capital as you prepare for a sale of the company - since the goal is to spend it only in ways which will impress just a few companies. Cash spent on activities which do not burnish your attractiveness is cash squandered as you prepare for the sale.

Buyers, especially strategic buyers, pay premiums over book or shareholder value. That premium is your focus. And it can only be truly determined once the buyer's wire transfer appears in your account.

When you were just commencing commercial sales and refining your business model to achieve positive cash flow, you were focusing on survival. Now, the sooner you can allocate your cash and activities toward impressing targeted strategic bidders, the sooner that beautiful wire transfer will arrive in your bank account.

Nothing commands a higher multiple than hope!
By David Steakley

You may recall that earlier in this book, I explained the definition of an inciting incident, using the movie industry and its story telling as the model. The inciting incident in a movie is the event at the beginning of the story that causes the hero's life to be completely transformed and irrevocably changed, and makes the whole story unfold.

I thought of this in a recent liquidity event in one of my portfolio companies. The company provides identity theft protection, and took a large round from a private equity firm, which returned about eight times investment in cash to the early angels, and still left them with all their stock in the deal, an outstanding result. The CEO did an absolutely masterful job in this transaction. The key to this was: *Nothing commands a higher multiple than hope.* The company had done very well, growing revenue rapidly, and demonstrating excellent results in several diverse sales channels> It had refined its offerings to the point where its service was the clear market leader. So with that tail wind behind, let's quickly bring in the freshly minted MBA to calculate the present value of the discounted future cash flows, and cash in!

Not so fast. The company had a number of potentially huge, blockbuster deals in progress. No one could say what these deals could be worth, or even whether they would ever be consummated. But, they were clearly mouthwatering. This prospect was what enabled the company to command a multiple of revenue so high that I first thought it had to be a typo. As we often hear, "You don't sell the steak, you sell the sizzle."

When you're selling your company, you have to work hard on your story, and the story doesn't really begin until the inciting incident.

Exit timing and price depends on many factors.
By Basil Peters

Selling an entire company is similar to selling shares in the public markets – how much you can get depends on how the company is doing, but also on how the overall market is behaving. For many stocks, the overall market is a bigger factor than how the company is actually doing at any point in time.

This 'external effect' is even more pronounced when an entire company is being sold because the market for companies is much less 'efficient.'

At the end of 2008, near the bottom of the debt bubble collapse, the overall stock market had dropped about 50%. If there was a similar index for the value of entire companies being sold, I am sure it would have gone down much farther than that, and stayed near the lows much longer. This is, in part, because the market for entire companies is much less 'efficient' and therefore more susceptible to changes in sentiment and liquidity.

How Long Does It Take to Sell a Company? Depending on whom you ask, and whether they are trying to sell you something, you will get different answers on how long it takes to sell a company.

The time to exit depends a lot on the company – primarily on how long it will take to get the company into a saleable state, and then how much time the senior team has available to work with the M&A advisor.

A good rule of thumb is that it will take six to eighteen months from making the decision to completing the sale. Therefore, in order to execute the best exit, the decision to sell has to be made that long before achieving the peak in corporate value.

Timing your exit – Don't ride it over the top.
By Basil Peters

Most entrepreneurs wait too long to start thinking about their exit. They usually sell their companies for much less than they could have.

That's exactly what I did in my first company. It was the first time I lost several million dollars, and the first of many similarly expensive – and valuable – lessons about exits.

Most of the technology companies I've known well exited too late. Yes, most. *Riding it over the top* is by far the most common exit scenario. The primary cause is simply our fundamental human nature.

I recently met with two bright entrepreneurs who are building a company in an exciting niche market riding on a long term trend. These two young founders chose their space well and were already global leaders in their niche. They had prototypes in the market and a respectable global mind share.

Their niche was heating up quickly – unfortunately for them. In the previous six months, I'd read several articles in finance blogs or newsletters about yet another company that had just been financed in their specific vertical. Most of the financings I read about were for $5 million to $20 million. In contrast, this local company had been built on something around $1 million in equity.

This is a scenario I've seen about a hundred times before - too much money flushing into a space the VCs think will be hot. Too many companies being founded with exactly the same business plan.

These entrepreneurs were too young to attract the amount of capital they'd need to compete in this new environment. They had only two strategic options – an early exit, or hiring a 'name CEO' that might be able to raise a big enough round in time. I recommended an exit because I knew the money flowing in to their space would also increase valuations – possibly by 2x to 5x over normal ranges.

You can probably guess the young entrepreneurs wanted to wait a 'little longer.'

I don't want to be too hard on these young entrepreneurs. They were mostly victims of their own human nature.

They just couldn't think about selling because they were having too much fun. They were leaders in their market and big companies were enquiring about huge orders. They knew their revenues were getting ready to grow – and possibly explode.

Unfortunately, they couldn't appreciate that it was also the absolute best time to sell their company. In fact, they should have started the exit process six to twelve months earlier.

Human nature also affects the buyers. They will always pay the most when everything is going perfectly and the future looks even brighter. The buyers' human nature also means that a skilled M&A advisor can usually sell for a lot more based on the 'promise' rather than the 'reality.'

And human nature works against the entrepreneurs on the downside. This one ends up costing most entrepreneurs and their investors a lot of money, because most of the time CEOs and boards wait until it's pretty clear that the company's value has peaked before starting the exit process. By the time the buyers get to serious price negotiations, it's also clear to them that the company's best days are behind it. And another six to eighteen months have passed, usually allowing the trend to extend even further.

With exits, like many things in business and life, timing can be (almost) everything.

Turning out the lights is a type of exit.
By Dave Berkus

In my life as an early stage investor, I've been closely involved with so many businesses, there were bound to be numerous stories of failures, hopefully from which to learn lessons for all of us as we go forward.

Several times in my investing life, as the final board member making the arrangements to dispose of remaining assets, I have literally been the one to turn out the lights, carry out the books and records to my car, and become the only remaining contact between the failed business and the investors, bankruptcy court, or creditors.

In aviation circles, we read in our pilot magazines about "Never again!" or "I learned about flying from that." Pilot-authors tell their stories in the first person, and all of us readers slow down to think while reading of these events, wondering "what if" or whether this could happen to me. And if it did, would I have reacted differently? Most importantly, we think: 'Now that I know this, would I behave differently if it did happen to me?'

So that is why we devote the next several insights to just this subject. Professional investors rarely attach a red letter upon a failed entrepreneur. In fact, if that person can tell his or her story and relate the lessons learned clearly, there is a positive response many of us will make to the next pitch from that person.

We who invest look for patterns from previous experience. Some of those patterns help us to spot and avoid problems we have seen play out in the past, often to disastrous conclusion. We learn to worry over obsolete inventory, too rapid hiring, failure to spot industry trends that make an offering less attractive, and so much more. Most of us can tell specific stories of losses that led to these expensive and gut-wrenching lessons.

In past insights, we have explored many aspects of preparation for and execution of a great exit. Let's spend a few cycles learning from the words of an eloquent, driven entrepreneur as he tells first hand his story of his failed business, followed by an analysis by yet another entrepreneur who knew the first, adding valuable insight about the problems, the failure to act upon trends, and more.

My story and what I learned from losing it all.
By Eric Greenspan

Eleven years and eight months of commitment, my life savings, every available dollar on every credit card, line and loan, and a promise to my children of a future, all gone. The real story behind my company's demise isn't exciting. It's simply about a team of dedicated individuals that failed.

We failed because the industry we were in changed over the years. We failed because the economy drastically fell into recession, particularly in the consumer sector. We failed because Apple invented the iPad and the Genius Bar. We failed because Microsoft finally got Windows right. We failed because we tried. We gave it everything we had and it in turn, it took everything we had.

Ours was an amazing company. With over 38,000 cult-like testimonials, one cannot dispute the company delivered a valuable service in a way like no other company has come close. Sadly, it will probably not be remembered this way.

As co-founder and CEO, I take responsibility. In doing so, I will assume all of the personally guaranteed loans and lines granted to the company. I personally guaranteed these loans, because I believed we could not fail. I was wrong.

The company had been forced to lower its prices, to meet competition and find acceptance. Additionally, over the years margins got smaller and eventually, stopped making sense. We worked tirelessly to find solutions to maintaining growth and profitability, critical components of any business.

The company was always seeking capital. As an entrepreneur, my greatest lesson learned here was how difficult it is to find capital for a services business. Venture capital firms have a distaste for the smaller multiples earned by services businesses, along with the challenge to scale such a business. As a result, the company was always under-capitalized.

For three years, the company paid its own bills. We were cash flow positive and we believed we could maintain this trend indefinitely. But then, new customers slowed, appointment bookings slowed and average appointment time dropped. The company raised some capital to supplement, shifted its business model, reduced its overhead, and sought new lines of business. During this period, the greatest opportunity in the company's history came into play. We were exuberant about a new relationship with a retail giant, which could offer our computer repair and installation services through their stores. We expected significant growth and anticipated the company to emerge as solvent, profitable and wildly successful. This didn't happen, but it also wasn't the end.

In May of our last year in operation, sales dropped drastically. After a solid April, we figured this was just the cycles of business. We sought capital just in case. Then June came and the downward trend continued. We continued to seek capital, launched aggressive discounted promotions and forged ahead.

Then, we got a verbal yes on a decent capital investment. We worked towards closing it. Sales remained sluggish during this period, but we were not giving up. We'd been here before, but never with an opportunity like the retail distribution contract with a big box chain, using their significant website, sitting in our lap. We were certain the funding would come through. Days went by; we stayed focused. Meanwhile, we were working on the big box retail store launch. We were so close to getting the funding. We needed it badly.

The leasing company wanted a payment. In a few days, our payroll that we had never missed in our eleven years was at risk. On that same Friday, our insurance lapsed, and we were forced to ground the fleet of 31 cars. Then came the weekend; our lease payment and payroll were both due Monday. On Sunday, around noon, the investor backed out. We immediately informed our board and shareholders that we were forced to halt operations. Monday came and the leasing company arrived to take our fleet. We missed payroll. It was over.

I immediately called every press outlet to be proactive in telling our story, changed our website to inform our customers; and our few remaining staff fielded calls and emails from our customers. There wasn't much more we could do.

Did we make mistakes along the way? You bet we did; plenty of them. But we learned and we grew and we fought against the current. At the end of the day, I'm not sure it would've mattered. The trend of self-healing, do-it-yourself installations and solid state devices will only make matters worse for our competitors. Apple changed the world.

Profit from the lessons learned from total loss.
By Eric Rhoads

We all know how hard EG and his team worked. They thought of every angle and attacked each with vigor. At the end of the day the team faced something every business faces, and often we're too close or too stubborn to see: *change.* Yes of course the economy had an impact as it has with all of us. Yet sometimes a bad economy reveals what a good economy masks. Great sales can hide problems. Poor sales make us pay close attention to our pennies, which we should be doing all along.

The greatest challenge a small business owner can face is that change happens fast. We often cling to our ideas that work, and refuse to adjust because we think the trend we're seeing is a result of something else (the economy for instance). When we see some success, we tend to increase our payrolls before we really should, and the biggest mistake is thinking more money will solve our problems. Sometimes having lots of capital simply speeds us up, so we hit the wall more quickly.

Having been in this position and barely squeaking buy on three different occasions, I can tell you that EG is feeling a tremendous amount of pain at the moment and he's probably frightened about how to raise his family and possibly fearful about whether or not to do this again.

America is full of great business guys like him who have been slammed down. The smart ones realize that this is the greatest experience of their careers, and that this experience will lead them to success if they are smart enough to examine what went wrong.

The first and most important thing is to accept the blame and not blame it on circumstances. Sure, circumstances played a role, but it's the nimble CEO who watches her or his money, trends, sales, and business acceleration, and is willing to slam on the breaks at high speed and make a sudden left turn, and hope it's the right decision. Though employees usually will tell you all the reasons you're wrong, most entrepreneurs and managers making quick decisions will tell you that anything good they did was met with employee resistance.

EG is a brilliant guy who will pick himself up, dust off the pain, and understand there is no shame in having to close a company. Though it's hard to recover, hard to face investors, hard to face family, it's important to clear his head of the angst caused by this tragedy and start working on the next idea.

The average multi-millionaire will tell you that he or she has failed two or three times before becoming successful. Failure is nothing more than a tool for growth. There is no shame in failure, and just like steel, strengthened by fire, EG and others like him will be better, stronger entrepreneurs or managers because of this experience.

When this first success happened to me I started living large. I was driving a car I thought I could afford. I was working on plans for a mega-house. I was spending more than I should and hiring more people than I should because I thought it would last, and thought I was a genius - until the day my bookkeeper told me "Eric, you'll be bankrupt in about six weeks." Thank Goodness I had six weeks, and rather than denial I immediately terminated fifty people and reduced to a staff of four.

Advisors told me I would be better off to just close the business because there was no way I could survive. It was painful, the start of a very long dry period. We almost did not make it with only four to do the work of many more. But we got through it, and when we came out of it we were stronger, and realized that we never needed that many people. We were forced to reinvent and develop ways to become more efficient and then became highly profitable.

I like and respect EG, and I wish he did not have to go through this. But perhaps it's the best thing that can happen to a young business owner early their career. It will make him stronger, and if he avoids the traps of allowing expenses to creep up in the future, he will be just fine.

Sell when growth is high, even if cash flow is low.
By John Huston

There are only two types of companies -those which have achieved positive cash flow and those which have not. *(Earnings Before Interest, Taxes, Depreciation and Amortization, or EBITDA is the most commonly used definition of cash flow.)*

While it is easy to divide all companies into just these two groups, this simplification ignores whether management has made a conscious, strategic choice about their growth. Perhaps you have decided to continue growing top line revenues at the expense of cash flow (EBITDA.) For high growth ventures being groomed for a lucrative liquidity event, this is usually a wise choice, presuming additional growth capital can be successfully raised on agreeable terms.

The issue is whether your company could pare back expenses and live within the cash it is currently generating - if you had to do so. This should be a major milestone goal of all start-ups. Until it is reached, survival still hinges on the kindness of outside funding sources.

But this too is an overly simplistic view. Usually leading up to the time positive cash flow is initially reached, the management team is not taking a market wage, payables are stretched, and any slowing of receivables collections would likely cause layoffs. The team knows their current expenses are being so closely managed, that at some point they would be unable to continue in this mode. They have achieved a level of cash generation which enables "survival" - but it is not sustainable.

Now that you are more mature as a business, management can decide how to balance building revenues versus building cash flow. There is a point at which building cash flow above revenues yields diminishing investor returns considering the amount of capital and time it consumes. Furthermore, having substantial positive cash flow may sub-optimize investor returns at the exit. This is because potential acquirers often act like mere financial buyers when they see a significant positive cash flow stream. This prompts them to merely apply a multiple (often 5 – 8X) to the EBITDA or cash flow of the business, always a smaller number than when pricing an acquisition for strategic reasons. So, rarely will this strategy or outcome enable investors to reap their target in a sale.

Ventures which have negative EBITDA, *but could turn it positive if they chose to do so*, are exhibiting the growth which attracts more bidders. Those which generate high returns at the exit are often not sporting positive cash flow when sold, *but they could dial back to be positive if required.* They are demonstrating by their actions that bidders cannot bid low, because by bidding low buyers would be assuming that a sale is necessary due to the company's negative cash flow.

The bottom line: Looking at best example companies in a sale, their acquisition strategy was to avoid growing their cash flow before the exit. Counterintuitive perhaps, but demonstrated to be effective.

Solve partnership issues before the company sale.
By William de Temple

This is a story about a company I became involved with, preparing for a sale as a way to resolve conflicts between two brothers who couldn't agree on how to manage their business.

The company was just three years old, already managing $7 million in revenues, and generating 23% in net income. And the company was in chaos. The company was structured as an LLC with each brother owning half interest. Three years before, they had self-incorporated to save a few dollars.

The older brother was the more experienced, having built a previous business to nearly $6 million before the 2008 recession wiped out that business. He was focused upon growth, reinvestment of profit, and special handling of employees as a prime asset. The younger brother had been a car dealer, treating his sales people like disposable assets, and unwilling to spend upon infrastructure or employee benefits.

The two brothers could not agree on much of anything. The rift between them grew so wide that the older brother refused to come into the office when the younger brother was present. It appeared that only a sale of the company could solve the growing problem of complete disagreement about management style and spending decisions. So I was brought in to prepare the company for sale.

As I began doing my due diligence to prepare a sales package, I found most everything I needed was missing. There was no membership agreement. The employee records were shoddy at best. They were keeping their books on a weekly basis rather than a monthly basis, making it difficult to do year to year comparisons. And they pulled out the bulk of the profits on a weekly basis rather than drawing a salary or declaring a distribution before year end. Nearly all the equipment had been brought over from the older brother's previous company and had never been recorded on the books of the new company.

It took much additional time and money to begin to bring the company into a place where it could be offered for sale. Unfortunately, this is not a unique story. It takes little extra effort to maintain generally acceptable accounting records, to incorporate without errors, and to keep a clean record of assets. These two paid the price for not doing so with an extended sales cycle and many months of continued tension between them, all of which was avoidable with a bit of pre-planning at the start of the relationship.

Don't be greedy even if you can.
By Dave Berkus

Sometimes the end game or sale of the company is not a happy event for the early investors, including the entrepreneur or the founders. Especially when outside investors, venture capitalists or angels have put in substantial money, and the sales price is not enough to give them a reasonable return for the time and money invested, these investors can be – in a word – greedy.

Most sophisticated investors will take either a promissory note or preferred stock, both of which come before founder or management stock in a sale or liquidation. Promissory notes come before any equity, and most late equity investments come before early equity investments, even of the same class of security. This makes for some head-rubbing when attempting to calculate the return on investment with a proposed sale. Further, preferred stock holders can be recipient of accrued dividends in a sale or liquidation. A rather common but small dividend rate of six percent becomes a massive amount after seven years, almost half again the value of the original investment. And some preferred investors have participation rights, where they take all of the above amounts, and then also convert their shares into common stock and participate again alongside the founders and option holders.

It is in this combination of possible methods of amassing a return that greed can become a significant factor, so much so that the courts are sometimes stepping in to void some of the most onerous terms of investment agreements when challenged by those locked out of payment in a sale.

Take a situation where the VC investors finally see the chance of a return after ten years, with participating preferred and fifty percent of the ownership after several rounds. A marginal sale at twice their original invested amount could yield a starting value of eighty percent of the sales price to the VCs (fifty percent invested plus accumulated dividends for ten years at six percent which equals thirty percent of the sale price) and then fifty percent of the remaining twenty percent after participation. The result is that the preferred shareholders would receive ninety percent of a sales price that was double their investment, compared to ten percent shared by the founders and all others, including option holder-employees.

No-one complains if the sales price is ten times the investment, since there is plenty to go around. It is in these marginal sales that the formula distorts returns so badly in favor of the investors.

Fortunately, and perhaps because the courts have not looked favorably upon these outcomes, many VCs will voluntarily forgive either accumulated dividends or participation in a marginal sale, especially if the sale is cultivated, planned and carried out by the efforts of the common shareholders including the founders.

Although many VCs are openly against allocating a "cutout" for management in marginal sales, practically speaking, management must be taken care of in marginal sales, or the sale might not happen at all. In a cutout, some percentage, usually fifteen or twenty percent of the total sale, is allocated to management in order to continue operations through the closing period and help in closing the sale. That further reduces the amount available to founders if not still in the ranks of management.

So this advice is directed to the investors. *Don't be greedy even if you can.* You will not be moving your IRR needle enough by grabbing a few extra dollars in a marginal sale, but you will incur the wrath of a number of stakeholders who would be more than willing to spread the word far and wide about your greedy ways. And that reputation will last for a long time in the entrepreneurial community.

Conversely, I have praised and seen others praise VCs who volunteer to eliminate participation clauses even before knowing the ultimate sales price in a deal. It is those who receive the loudest accolades since they have given up a right for the good of the rest of the investor and management community.

Take the time to celebrate your exit.
By Dave Berkus

We come to the end of this book of insights with a thought about how you might view your successful exit from the company you have spent so much effort to build.

You've worked hard for years to reach the payoff, and the money sure looks good as you contemplate the wire transfer to come, and then watch your bank account fill to a level you only dreamed of during those rough cash flow years. You might even allow yourself to admit that you almost lost it all several times during this long run, and that only you knew how close you came to the abyss. But you did make it, and that's what counts.

Whether the exit was as large as you hoped, or whether your goals of taking care of all the people who helped you get to this point were realized, the exit itself generates a complex set of emotions in all of us.

First there comes a sense of relief, knowing that you no longer need to worry over daily cash or threats to your net worth. Then you experience a feeling of guilt when you realize that not all of your early associates share the same outcome, either financially or perhaps with their continued employment with the buyer.

Then you focus on the money in your bank account, smiling at the accomplishment of accumulating assets that are tangible and can be valued, perhaps for the first time.

But what most entrepreneurs fail dramatically at is to celebrate the moment. To celebrate with those who took the journey with you, with those closest to you who sacrificed as you spent those long hours away. To celebrate with your suppliers who helped you, especially during the rough times. To celebrate with your customers, who worry over continuity and look to you for assurances that the transition will not negatively affect them. And to celebrate for yourself, for making it all the way to the finish line.

Not many founders or entrepreneurs do experience the success of a favorable sale of the business they dreamed would make them rich. Many fail multiple times. Some fail in the first year of the attempt. Others are diluted by subsequent investors to the point where there was nothing for them to celebrate at all in a sale.

So as you prepare to turn over the reins to another; to separate from a business that has become a part of your being, it is time to think of nothing but the good done, the examples set, the positive company culture you leave behind.

As you begin to focus upon the future, remember the emotions, the lessons, the lasting friendships from the past. I often advise managers, CEOs and entrepreneurs always to part on a positive note and never burn the bridges of any past relationship. You'll never guess whom you'll meet in your next act, and how they will be able to contribute positively to your next success.

So celebrate your exit by reaching out to as many of those who've helped along the way as you can. Close this chapter of your life on the highest note possible. Take a long breath. The do as all good entrepreneurs do. Start dreaming of the next big idea. Take with you the best wishes from those in your past, and build upon the education you received with this effort.

Write a book; I did. Write a long hand letter to someone who helped you make it to the finish line. That extra effort will shock and please them. Call an early key employee and take that person to dinner as a thank you for those hard times.

Hit the beach.   Pay attention to your family.   Think about investments and tax efficiency. Go into a mental dark room and dream about your next act. Take a long breath, or weeks of long breaths. Exhale slowly. This is what a moment of reduced pressure and responsibility feels like. Savor that moment.

Then if it strikes you as right, start the process all over again. May you have only the greatest success in your next act, whatever that is and wherever it takes you.

About the author/editor...

Dave Berkus has a proven track record in operations, venture investing and corporate board service, both public and private. As an entrepreneur, he has formed, managed and sold successful businesses in the entertainment and software arenas. As a private equity investor, he has obtained healthy returns from liquidity events in over a dozen investments in early-stage ventures. As a corporate mentor and director, he was named *"Director of the Year"* for his directorship efforts with over 40 companies in the past decade.

Dave was the founder of **Computerized Lodging Systems Inc.,** *(CLS),* which he guided as founder and CEO for over a decade that included two consecutive years on the *Inc.500* list of America's fastest growing companies, expansion to six foreign subsidiaries and twenty-nine foreign distributors while capturing 16% of the world market for his enterprise products. Known as a hospitality industry visionary with many "firsts" to his credit and for his accomplishments in advancing technology in the hospitality industry, in 1998 he was inducted into the **Hospitality (HFTP) "International Hall of Fame"**, one of only thirty so honored worldwide over the years.

He has made over 90 investments in early stage ventures, for which he has an IRR of 97%, which includes returns from his two funds (**Berkus Technology Ventures, LLC** and **Kodiak Ventures, L.P.**, for which he is the managing partner). He is also Chairman Emeritus of the Tech Coast Angels, one of the largest angel networks in the United States.

In recognition for adding significant shareholder value for emerging technology companies over the past decade, he was named *"Director of the Year-Early Stage Businesses"* by the *Forum for Corporate Directors* of Orange County, California and *"Technology Leader of the Year"* by the Los Angeles County Board of Supervisors. Dave currently sits on ten corporate boards and four non-profit boards.

Dave is also a senior partner in the twenty year old consulting firm of *Hospitality Automation Consultants, LTD (HACL)*, and lends his considerable visionary and strategic talents to worldwide hospitality vendors, hotel chains and management groups. He is the partner responsible for business process reorganization, strategic planning, wide-area network infrastructure, and enterprise management systems.

A graduate of Occidental College, Dave is a long time Trustee of the College. Aside from this book, he is author of *"BERKONOMICS"* and its accompanying workbook, *"Advanced BERKONOMICS," "Extending the Runway,"* and co-author of *"Better than Money!"* all books for emerging growth technology company executives. Dave serves as Board Member of the San Gabriel Valley Council, *Boy Scouts of America*, is a former board member of the *Forum for Corporate Directors,* and is Chairman of the Advisory Board of *ABL/TECHNOLOGY*, a networking organization of CEOs in high tech businesses.

He is often engaged as keynote speaker for events worldwide, speaking on trends in technology, of entrepreneurial or investor lessons from BERKONOMICS, and of legal and practical issues of governance for emerging company corporate boards.

To contact Mr. Berkus for speaking engagements or workshops, email dberkus@berkus.com **, or phone (626)355-5375.**

Dave's books are available for purchase from the above website, or the same source as this book was purchased.

Subscribe to the free weekly email or blog, www.Berkonomics.com, containing slices of information from Dave's books with lots of comments from readers with their own stories to tell.

Follow Dave on Twitter (@daveberkus) and Facebook (Dave.Berkus).

Other books by Dave Berkus available directly from *www.berkus.com* or from your favorite bookseller or online store:

EXTENDING THE RUNWAY
Hard cover edition only

The five tools board members and executives can use to help their companies succeed. How boards and CEOs should relate to each other for growing the enterprise. Fifty-eight critical questions boards and management should consider in order to assure their mutual alignment.

BERKONOMICS
Hard cover, soft cover and eBook editions

The central volume in this series. One hundred and one critical insights for entrepreneurs, CEOs and board members covering the life of the company from ignition through liquidity event. Dave tells over fifty stories to illustrate his insights, culled from his experience as entrepreneur and service on over forty corporate and ten non-profit boards.

BERKONOMICS WORKBOOK

Companion to BERKONOMICS, this very personal journal contains 101 exercises for the CEO or manager that make each of the insights contained in BERKONOMICS come to life in the form of provocative and actionable questions to be answered right on the pages of the workbook. Once completed, this workbook becomes a personal blueprint for business growth.

ADVANCED BERKONOMICS
Hard cover, soft cover and eBook editions

Volume two of this series. One hundred and one critical insights for entrepreneurs, CEOs and board members covering the life of the company from ignition through liquidity event. More advanced insights into planning and measurement for success with small business startups.

SMALL BUSINESS SUCCESS SERIES
A Series of eight short and inexpensive books or eBooks

Take all the great material in BERKONOMICS and ADVANCED BERKONOMICS and slice it by subject, and you'll have these eight inexpensive, short books about issues that you and your management team needs to focus upon today. Ideal for giving to your entire management group for group discussions and business planning sessions.

BOOKS and eBOOKS IN THIS SERIES:

1. Starting up!
2. Raising Money
3. Positioning for Success
4. Managing your Workforce

5. Protecting your Business
6. Growing your Business
7. Building Great Boards
8. Cashing Out!